TINPANAlley

Routledge Popular Music

A series of books for schools edited by
Graham Vulliamy and Edward Lee

TIN PAN ALLEY

John Shepherd

Routledge & Kegan Paul
London, Boston and Henley

To my nieces
Anne and Susan Shepherd

First published in 1982
by Routledge & Kegan Paul
39 Store Street, London WC1E 7DD,
9 Park Street, Boston, Mass. 02108, USA and
Broadway House, Newtown Road,
Henley-on-Thames, Oxon RG9 1EN
Set in 11 on 14 pt Helvetica by
Input Typesetting Ltd, London
and printed in Great Britain by
St Edmundsbury Press
Bury St Edmunds, Suffolk
© John Shepherd 1982

ISBN 0-7100-0904-6

Contents

1 'How to write a popular song'

If you had walked down some of the streets surrounding New York's Union Square in the summer of 1900, your ears would have met with a strange sound. Summer in New York is very hot. It is also very humid, and you are likely to sweat just standing still. And because there was no air-conditioning in 1900, office windows were kept open to bring what little relief there was from the stifling heat.

The people who worked in many of the offices near Union Square were in a very interesting business. They were professional song-writers. Their job was to write songs which would sell to the public in great numbers, and so make a lot of money for the publishers who printed them.

Because they were paid by the publishers for their work the song-writers had to be very good at their job. But they were seldom very good as pianists. Talking about fellow song-writer George Meyer, for example, famous 'Alleyman' Irving Caesar said: 'I wrote quite a few songs with George Meyer . . . Great song writer, but he, too, couldn't play the piano. He was one-fingered – well, almost one-fingered. But he was a great melodist.'

Though they usually played with only one finger, the song-writers did not always hit the right note, and the piano was quite often out of tune. With dozens of them working during the summer, with windows open, there was an amazing jangle of sound. 'It's always reminded me of kitchen clatter, just like tin pans,' remarked famous song-writer Harry von Tilzer. For this reason the area became known as 'Tin Pan Alley'.

Tin Pan Alley was the beginning of the 'pop' music industry as we know it today, and it is this industry that will be explored in this book. But first, it is necessary to find out how these song-writers went about writing their songs. How did they decide what the songs were going to be about? And how did they get ordinary people to buy them?

The sentimental ballad

In order to sell in big numbers, a song had to become popular with a great many Americans. To do this, of course, it had to have words and music which Americans thought good. But a song also had to do one of three other things. It had to be written in a musical style that was in fashion at the time. It had to be about something that was in the public's mind. Or it had to appeal to the public's emotions.

Tin Pan Alley has always been quick to take over and change different musical styles for its own ends if it thought there was money to be made. The most important of these styles have come from the music of black Americans. The first to be used by Tin Pan Alley – ragtime – is described in chapter 3. Another – jazz – is discussed in chapter 5.

Tin Pan Alley has also been quick to write songs about topical events which were in the public's mind. New inventions were quite often celebrated in song, for example. In 1901, at a time when the telephone was becoming more and more common, Charles K. Harris wrote 'Hello, Central, Give me Heaven'. (The

word 'Central' refers to the telephone exchange.)
Two songs, 'Up, Up, Up, in My Aeroplane' (1909)
and 'Come, Josephine, in My Flying Machine' (1910),
followed the first successful flights by the Wright
brothers in 1903. Topical songs did not have to be
about new inventions, however. They could, for
example, be about the death of a famous person. So
when silent-movie star Rudolph Valentino died, in
1926, Jimmy McHugh wrote 'There's a New Star in
Heaven Tonight'.

But the most important kind of song to be
produced in Tin Pan Alley at this time was the song
which appealed to the public's emotions. This is
known as the sentimental ballad. The sentimental
ballad had been popular with Americans during the
nineteenth century, and it came to be the mainstay of
the Alley's output. Although many kinds of music
(such as ragtime and jazz) have come and gone
during the history of Tin Pan Alley, the sentimental
ballad has always been there. This is as true now as
it was in 1900, when the well-known song 'A Bird in
a Gilded Cage' became extremely popular. A good
example of a modern ballad is Paul McCartney's
'Yesterday', which was written in 1965.

Like countless other ballads, 'A Bird in a Gilded
Cage' tells a story. This one is about a beautiful
young woman who married an older man for his
money. It goes as follows:

The ballroom was fill'd with fashion's throng,
It shone with a thousand lights,
And there was a woman who passed along,
The fairest of all the sights;
A girl to her lover then softly sighed,
'There's riches at her command,'
'But she married for wealth, not love,' he cried,
'Tho' she lives in a mansion grand.'

The beautiful woman surveyed the scene,
Her flatterers by the score,
Her gems were the purest, her gown divine,
So what could a woman want more.
But memory brings back the face of a lad,
Whose love she had turned aside,
But happiness cannot be bought with gold,
Altho' she's a rich man's bride.

I stood in a church-yard just at eve,
When sunset adorned the west,
And looked at the people who'd come to grieve,
For lov'd ones now laid at rest.
A tall marble monument mark'd the grave,
Of one who'd been fashion's queen,
And I thought she is happier here at rest,
Than to have people say, when seen,

[chorus]
She's only a bird in a gilded cage,
A beautiful sight to see,
You may think she's happy and free from care,
She's not tho' she seems to be,
'Tis sad when you think of her wasted life,
For youth cannot mate with age,
And her beauty was sold for an old man's gold,
She's a bird in a gilded cage.

If you have read Ed Lee's *Folk Song and Music Hall*, you will know that ballads were sung for many centuries before 'Bird in a Gilded Cage' was written. They also told a story, but this song is different in some important ways; for these reasons it is called a sentimental ballad.

'Sentimental' is a word which has several meanings. The first of these is that the song is not really concerned with the story ('what happened next?'), so much as with 'sentiments' or emotions ('what did people feel?'). The word sentimental can also mean that the emotions felt are sad or melancholy. This is certainly true, because the song tells of the woman's memory of 'the face of a lad/ Whose love she had turned aside.' Although she has plenty of money, it cannot buy the very thing the woman has not got – love. In the end she is thought to be happier 'at rest' than to be alive and have people pointing out her mistake.

There is one other important meaning of the word 'sentimental' in this situation, which is that the song is full of 'sentimentality', that is, emotions which are unreal and idealised. The song's message is that 'happiness cannot be bought with gold.' In one way this is clearly true, just as it tends to be true that 'youth cannot mate with age.' But the song turns its back on the fact that young people's love is placed under huge and often impossible difficulties when they are desperately poor, as so many people were at that time. It is nice to believe that 'love is all you need' when love is all you *have*, but is it true?

Nevertheless, by dealing with subjects which matter to millions of people, in ways that they wanted to hear, this song illustrates the way in which Tin Pan Alley's influence was able to spread rapidly throughout the world. This point will be taken up again, especially in chapter 9.

One of the most common ingredients of sentimental songs is nostalgia, or the looking back at pleasant things that you can no longer have. The woman in the 'gilded cage' can no longer have love, for example, although she certainly once had the chance. Nostalgia still plays a part in sentimental songs. For instance, the opening of Paul McCartney's 'Yesterday' is as follows:

Yesterday all my troubles seemed so far away,
Now it looks as if they're here to stay,
Oh I believe in yesterday.

Here, the writer has lost his girl and is looking back to the time when 'all [his] troubles seemed so far away'.

The sentimental ballad's appeal to the public's emotions has not changed over the years. What has changed is the way the words and music make that appeal. One of the biggest changes took place in the late 1920s and early 1930s, and this is discussed in chapter 6.

Mass production

'A Bird in a Gilded Cage' was written by Harry von Tilzer. Tilzer was a quite remarkable Alleyman who wrote well over 3,000 songs (that's the same as writing a song every working day for about eleven-and-a-half years).

Harry von Tilzer was a little unusual in producing so many songs. But he was not unusual in the speed with which he could write them. Tin Pan Alley was in business to write songs in much the same way that Coca-Cola were in business to produce their soft drink. The faster the songs or the Coke could be produced, the more money there was to be made. So if you were a song-writer, you had to write fast. 'It may sound immodest,' said Irving Caesar, 'but you'd be amazed . . . that most of my songs that sold were written in less than fifteen minutes. "Tea for Two" was written in less than four minutes.' To be a professional you also had to be able to write a song at any time. 'Anyone could write a popular song that's no great shakes,' continued Caesar. 'But to be able to write a song at any time of day or night, that's what a pro had to be able to do. I wrote songs *any* time, on a bet.'

In order to write songs quickly, song-writers had to have a constant supply of titles, stories and lyrics. Sometimes the song-writers got their titles and stories directly from the people for whom they were writing, the public. It is said that one lyricist used to sit all night in a New York restaurant listening to other people's conversations. If he heard a funny remark or a catchy phrase he would write it down in his notebook for future use as a title. Again, the title for the 1923 hit song 'Yes, We Have No Bananas' is supposed to have come from a New York fruit seller who spoke little English. This kind of contact with the public was important for song-writers. Through it they made sure they were writing about things that were on the public's mind at the time.

Another way of getting stories for songs and keeping in touch with the public was to read the newspapers. In 1894, for example Edward B. Marks (a partner in the publishing house of Joseph W. Stern & Co.) happened to read a story about a lost child. The child had been found wandering the streets by a policeman who turned out to be the child's lost father. This was excellent material for a sentimental, tear-jerking ballad. Marks produced the lyrics, his partner Stern provided the music, and another hit song ('The Little Lost Child') had been written.

Tin Pan Alley was a tightly knit community. All its offices were in the same small area of New York, and everyone seemed to know everybody else. Tin Pan Alley also produced an enormous number of songs. For these reasons, one song often sounded much like another. A song-writer would hear a new song by someone else, and the melodies would sink into his head. Sometime later, when writing one of his own songs, these melodies would come out in a slightly altered version. Alternatively, the song-writer might use bits of older music that he had heard. A good example of this can be heard in 'Yes, We Have No Bananas.' If the song is listened to carefully it is possible to detect parts of 'The Hallelujah Chorus' in some places, and parts of 'My Bonnie Lies Over the Ocean' in others.

'Bananas' is also interesting in that several people helped to write it. In their haste to get a new song out, song-writers would willingly make use of any suggestions they received from their colleagues. So although Frank Silver and Irving Cohn are down as the writers of 'Bananas', they were in fact helped by (among others) James Hanley, Ballard McDonald and Lew Brown, as well as the famous publishers Maurice Shapiro and Louis Bernstein.

Because Tin Pan Alley quickly produced a great number of songs that often sounded alike, it can be said that the songs were 'mass produced'. But it was no good mass producing songs if the songs could not be sold as fast as they were written. So, besides mass production, Tin Pan Alley also needed 'professional marketing'.

**Profes-
sional
marketing**

Today, song-writers and music publishers make most of their money through the sale of records and from fees collected every time a record is played on the radio, the television, or in any public place (such as a disco). These fees are known as royalties.

But before the age of records and radio, music publishers made their money through the sale of sheet music. Sheet music contained just the vocal line and piano accompaniment of a song. It was played mainly by ladies on the pianos which were to be found in the parlours of most respectable middle-class homes.

Song-writers, on the other hand, made their money by selling a song to a publisher for a lump sum. For example, Charles Graham sold 'The Picture That Is Turned toward the Wall' to the famous publishing house of Witmark for $15.00 in 1891. Alternatively, the song-writer received royalties on each copy of the sheet music that was sold. Finally, some song-writers, such as Charles K. Harris and Harry von Tilzer, were their own publishers.

In order to get the public to buy their songs music publishers tried to get as much public exposure for them as possible. The best way of doing this was to get a well-known artist to sing the song in a vaudeville show (see chapter 2). So, in the early days of Tin Pan Alley, the publishers themselves used to travel round the vaudeville theatres in New York trying to persuade the artists to sing their songs. 'Sixty joints a week I used to make,' wrote Edward B. Marks. 'Joe Stern, my partner, covered about forty. What's more we did it every week.'

An important part of the persuasion was for the publisher to sing his song and then convince the artist that it was bound to be a hit. But the persuasion went beyond this. Publishers would buy drinks for artists and their bands in an attempt to get them to try a song, and would sometimes take them out for meals. Also, artists who agreed to push songs were frequently given royalties as if they were one of the song-writers. That is why the name of a star such as Al Jolson appears on the sheet music of a song as one of its writers when in fact the star had not helped to write the song at all. Sometimes, stars were given gifts by publishers. These could range from cars and race horses to yachts. There was a lot of money in the song-writing business.

When the publishing houses became established

(and this was by 1900), the publishers would stay in their offices and send out professional 'pluggers'. For example, the famous song-writer Irving Berlin started life working as a plugger for Harry von Tilzer's publishing house. Bing Crosby has described the visits of these professional pluggers. 'They'd come to your dressing room to demonstrate whatever song their company was concentrating on,' he said. 'They could sing and dance, they knew all the jokes. It was an amusing interlude. And they always had the same line: "Bing, I promise you, this is going to be the number one song, there's no question about it".'

But the publishers did not stop there. Once an artist had agreed to sing a song, they would often 'plant' someone in the theatre audience to jump up and repeat the song's chorus when the song had finished. The audience were meant to think that the 'plant' was one of their own number who had been overwhelmed by the music. The publisher hoped that the actions of the 'plant' would help to fix a song in the audience's mind, and so lead them to buy the sheet music. Song-writer Gus Edwards worked as a 'plant' when only a boy of fourteen.

Another way in which publishers plugged their music was to make a series of magic lantern slides. The slides, which were rather like present-day colour transparencies, told the story of a particular song. Because, at that time, there were few records and no 'talking pictures', the slides were shown during the interval in a motion-picture theatre while an entertainer led the audience in singing the song.

Publishers would in fact plug their songs anywhere they could find an audience. So pluggers were to be found singing their publisher's songs in music shops, department stores, restaurants, sports arenas, on street corners and on the backs of trucks. They were very colourful people and many stories have been told about them. It is difficult to know whether these tales are always true. However, one story is typical of the time. It is said that Jack Robbins (a sixteen-year-old plugger working in Chicago) got hold of a hay wagon, put on farmers' clothes and started driving down a busy main street. The song he was advertising was 'It's an Old Horse That Knows Its Way Home'.

By 1900 sentimental ballads and topical songs were being mass produced and professionally marketed in much the same way as Coca-cola, clothes and carpets. The idea was the same in each case. You found out what the public wanted and worked as hard as possible at selling it to them.

One song-writer had understood this idea as early as the 1880s. His name was Charles K. Harris. He had a small office on Grand Avenue in the town of Milwaukee, and outside this office there hung a sign. It read 'Songs Written to Order'.

In 1892, Harris wrote and published a sentimental ballad called 'After the Ball'. The song was an unprecedented success. In the end it sold over 10 million copies. With the money he made from this song Harris moved to New York and set up his own publishing company. He was sure that, like many other things, song-writing was a business that could be learnt by other people. So he wrote a book about it. The title of the book was *How to Write a Popular Song*.

Charles K. Harris was the father of Tin Pan Alley. But what exactly gave rise to this tightly knit community of commercial song-writers and publishers? This question is answered in the next chapter.

2 Travelling troupes and the growth of vaudeville

Nineteenth-century America

We nowadays have a great variety of entertainment at our fingertips. The push of a button will give us music on the radio or stereo, or a film on television. And, for the great numbers of people who live in or near big cities, visits to cinemas, theatres, restaurants and discos are easy.

But the ease with which we can get entertainment and be in touch with the rest of the world is recent. In the middle of the nineteenth century there were no radios, no televisions, no cinemas, no gramophones, no telephones, no cars and no aeroplanes. Even more important, there were fewer towns and cities, and they were not nearly as big as they are today. Towns and cities with populations over 100,000 are now quite common. But in 1860, there were only nine such cities in America (New York, Philadelphia, Boston, Baltimore, Brooklyn, New Orleans, Cincinnati, St Louis and Chicago). Furthermore, only one person in six lived in a town with a population of 8,000 or more. In 1840, the figure had been as low as one in twelve. So, unlike today, mid-nineteenth-century America was mainly a rural country dotted with small towns. It was also a country where travel and the spread of news was slow.

Tin Pan Alley came into being because of the growth in the size and importance of cities which took place between 1860 and 1900. And, as new means of communication were invented during the twentieth century, they were used by Tin Pan Alley to spread its message not only across the whole of America, but to other parts of the world as well. However, in the middle of the nineteenth century there were few big cities, there was no Tin Pan Alley, and there was no American entertainment industry with tentacles reaching to the four corners of the earth. So what did Americans do at this time for entertainment?

Although there was no Tin Pan Alley in mid-nineteenth-century America, there were music publishers. A great deal of the sheet music which they issued was sold to rural Americans over the counters of the general stores which were to be found in most small country towns. The music was then played and sung in people's homes, as well as in the churches, schoolrooms and meeting halls of local communities. At this time singing was the most common and most important kind of communal entertainment. So one answer to our question is that during the mid-nineteenth century many Americans entertained themselves with song.

Another answer is that they were entertained by travelling artists. Instead of the audience going to the artists, as it does today, the artists came to the audience. They came mainly in wagons, in showboats, and on the railroads which were springing up all over the midwest of America at this time. They also came in many different kinds of troupes. There were circuses, medicine men, singing families, theatrical groups and minstrel shows. But, whatever the kind of troupe, they nearly always carried 'variety' acts with them. The acts were put on by acrobats, jugglers, dancers, comedians and, of course, singers. In their different ways, *all* these acts needed music.

It was acts such as these which made up the 'circus concert'. This was a short entertainment given after the regular circus performance in another part of the big top. Also, the medicine men who travelled the country in wagons, selling alcoholic but otherwise useless medicines to the public, often had entertainers who travelled with them. As well as driving the wagon, it was the entertainer's job to attract an audience so that the medicine man could go about selling his remedies. Music formed a central part of this entertainment. Another outlet for entertainers was the showboats which steamed up and down the rivers of the midwest and carried variety acts.

Many of the musicians who toured America at this time were from Europe, and some had a background of English music hall. The best known of these European musicians were the Swedish soprano Jenny Lind and the English baritone Henry Russell. Russell's career is described by Ed Lee in *Folk Song and Music Hall*.

A lot of the songs published at this time are familiar to people today. Some, such as 'Battle Hymn of the Republic' (1862) and 'Marching through Georgia' (1865), grew out of the American Civil War of 1861–5. Others, such as 'I'll Take You Home Again, Kathleen' (1876), were standard sentimental ballads. But some, like 'Camptown Races' (1850), 'Oh! Susanna' (1848) and 'The Old Folks at Home' are altogether different. If you listen to any of these songs, you will notice that they have very snappy rhythms and that the lyrics are not in ordinary

Jenny Lind, the 'Swedish Nightingale'

English. The first four lines of 'The Old Folks at Home', for example, read like this:

Way down upon de Swannee ribber,
Far, far away,

THE OLD FOLKS AT HOME,

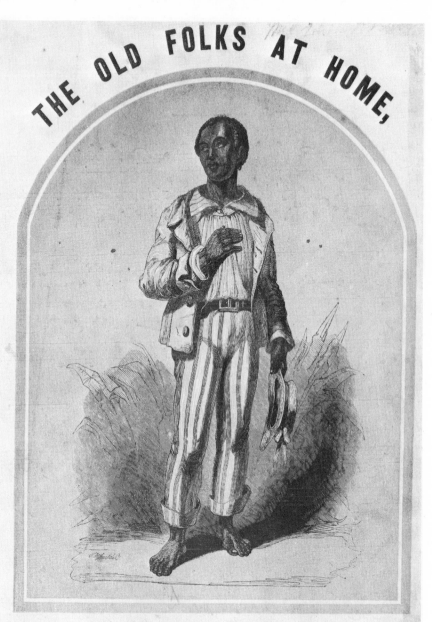

SONG AND CHORUS.

Ent. Sta. Hall.

THE MUSICAL TREASURY.

Price Threepence

LONDON: DAVIDSON, PETER'S HILL, DOCTORS' COMMONS, SOUTH OF ST. PAUL'S.

647

Dere's wha my heart is turning ebber,
Dere's wha de old folks stay.

All three of these songs were written by Stephen
Collins Foster (1826–64), the son of an army colonel.
Foster had spent four years (1846–50) working for a
river-boat agency in Cincinnati, and it was during this
time that he heard the singing of black boatmen.
What made these songs different was that they tried
to capture the language and music of black people.
Yet it is likely that the songs amounted to little more
than imitations.

Afro-American music

In his book *Jazz and Blues*, Graham Vulliamy
describes how, when black slaves were shipped
from West and Central Africa, they brought with them
their own kind of music. This was very different from
the European music of white Americans. When the
two types of music came into contact, another music
grew up that was neither purely African nor purely
European, but a mixture of both. This music is
known as 'Afro-American' music.

It is perhaps easiest to think of early Afro-
American music as developing in three main ways.
There were spirituals, the black man's religious
music, which resulted from the mixing of African
music and European hymns. There were the blues, a
soulful and melancholy music, which grew out of the
black man's adaptation of European ballads and folk
songs. Finally, there were the 'rags' or 'jigs' played at
the dances of black people. Rag or jig music
eventually became ragtime, the first Afro-American
music to be taken over by Tin Pan Alley.

Like the blues, rag or jig music sometimes
resulted from the mixing of African music with
European ballads and folk songs. The music also

frequently made use of European folk dances such as reels, schottisches and jigs (these are described by Ed Lee in *Folk Song and Music Hall*). Rags or jigs were also influenced by the music of white marching bands. These bands played at any big occasion: parades, funerals, marriages, picnics, baptisms, political meetings and so on.

Though they had to work very hard and were often badly treated, the black slaves usually had some time off on Sundays, and it was on Sundays that many dances were held. The most famous of the black dances was called the 'Cakewalk'. It was described as follows by the son of a freed slave, Shepherd N. Edmonds:

> The cakewalk was originally a plantation dance, just a happy movement they did to the banjo music because they couldn't stand still. It was generally on Sundays when there was little work that the slaves both young and old would dress up in hand-me-down finery to do a high-kicking, prancing walk-around. They did a take-off on the high manners of the white folks in the 'big house', but their masters, who gathered round to watch the fun, missed the point. It's supposed to be that the custom of a prize started with the master giving a cake to the couple that did the proudest movement.

Jump Jim Crow   In *Folk Song and Music Hall*, Ed Lee tells of a young white actor, Thomas Rice, who one day in the mid-1820s noticed an old and decrepit black man shuffling along, jumping and skipping in a most peculiar manner. While he did this, the black man hummed a ditty in which the words 'Jump Jim Crow' kept being repeated. Rice wrote a song which imitated the black man's words and music. He then put together an act in which he sang his song and copied the movements of the black man. He introduced the act to a Baltimore audience in 1828 and got a tumultuous reception. Very soon white performers right across the country were imitating black music and dance, and presenting it to white audiences. Black impersonators had become fashionable.

Early 'blackface' minstrel troupes were made up entirely of *white* artists who blacked their faces with burnt cork to look like black men. The troupes played only to white audiences. As the shows gradually took shape, different 'Negro' characters came into being. There was Mr Interlocutor, who would 'feed' lines for the jokes, puns and slapstick comedy of Mr Tambo and Mr Bones. Tradition had it that Mr Tambo was tall and thin, and Mr Bones short and fat. Later on there was Jim Dandy, the character who strutted in his finery to the music of the Cakewalk.

The slapstick comedy of Mr Interlocutor, Mr Tambo and Mr Bones made up the first part of the minstrel show. This ended in a grand review of the performers, called the 'walk around'. The 'walk around' was based upon the Cakewalk, which was described earlier. The second part of the minstrel show, or 'olio', consisted of variety acts in which the different artists could show off their individual talents. The show ended with the 'afterpiece'. This was usually a take off of a straight stage play which at the same time made quips about current affairs.

The white 'blackface' minstrels caricatured the songs, dances and jokes of the black plantation slaves in the same way that the slaves had poked fun at the habits and dress of their white masters in

"NUFFIN HURTS ME"
OR
SLEEP ON A COTTON-BALE-ROOST UP A TREE.

CHORUS. I like cheese, I like honey,
I'm not the boy to refuse any money,
I can sleep on a cotton bale, or roost up a tree,
I tell you what it is boys "NUFFIN HURTS ME".

WRITTEN BY
HARRY HUNTER,

COMPOSED BY
VINCENT DAVIES,

SUNG WITH THE GREATEST SUCCESS
BY
"THE CELEBRATED MOHAWK MINSTRELS",
AGRICULTURAL HALL, LONDON.

ENT. STA. HALL.

PRICE 3/-

London,
JOSEPH WILLIAMS, 24, BERNERS St W,
AND
123, CHEAPSIDE CORNER OF WOOD St EC.

the Cakewalk. On the whole, the caricatures of the 'blackface' minstrel shows were vicious and cruel, and set out to ridicule the black man as loose-limbed, awkward and simple-minded. The popular idea that many white people had of slaves at this time can be seen on the cover of 'Nuffin Hurts Me'. Here, the black man is portrayed as so simple-minded that he is content to 'sleep on a cotton bale or roost up a tree', and so loose-limbed that when he falls (through awkwardness) out of a tree onto the horns of a cow, he is not hurt.

The make-up of the minstrel troupes changed quite a lot after 1865, the year in which the slaves gained their freedom. After that, it was possible for them to form their own minstrel troupes. It might seem strange that black people should want to take part in shows which made fun of them in such a cruel way. However, it was far from easy for freed black slaves to find work, so anything that came along was welcome. Also, the black performers turned the tables on their white brethren by once again poking fun at them.

It would not have been possible for white and black people to keep poking fun at each other had their lives not been so different. The white plantation owners were very rich, of course, and the blacks who worked for them extremely poor. But on top of that whites and blacks lived and worked apart from each other (this came to be known as 'segregation'). Because most whites did not live and work among black people, they were able to believe that what they saw in the minstrel shows was a true picture of the lives of black people. And when black people poked fun at white people (either at black dances or in minstrel shows), many whites would have seen it as just another example of the awkwardness and

The black man caricatured as sub-human in a minstrel show

simple-mindedness of black people. After all, the blacks would not have been thought clever enough to caricature whites. That is why the laugh was nearly always on the whites.

Although minstrel shows painted an untrue picture of black people, they did prepare the way for white acceptance of black music and dance towards the end of the nineteenth century. But it was because the minstrel shows *did* paint an untrue picture that the black music and dance accepted by whites was never quite the same as that of the blacks themselves. For example, the ragtime enjoyed by white audiences between the late 1890s and the First World War was very different to the ragtime being played in black communities.

Vaudeville

The previous section of this chapter has described how mid-nineteenth-century America was a largely rural country which either entertained itself or was entertained by different kinds of travelling artists. But by 1900 the picture had changed dramatically. This was due mainly to a big increase in population.

However, this growth in population was not split evenly between the country and the cities. While the rural population of America doubled between 1860 and 1900, that of the towns and cities grew to four times the size. As we have seen, only one in six people lived in a town with a population of over 8,000 in 1860. By 1900 that figure was one in three. New York, which in 1860 had had a population of 800,000, now had one of 2,500,000. The population of Memphis went from 23,000 to 100,000 in the same period. And by 1920 there were more people living in towns with populations of over 8,000 than were living in the country.

During this time, America changed from having a

mainly rural or farming economy to having one that was basically industrial. A much greater emphasis was now placed on making goods which could be sold at home and abroad for profit. It was this promise of money which drew many people (both black and white) from the country to work in the factories of big cities. The great numbers of people who were now packed into the small areas of the cities needed entertainment as a relief from the drudgery of this factory work. The entertainment was provided by variety shows which took as their model the shows put on in British music halls.

The variety shows which were put on in the theatres of big towns and cities for white people grew out of the 'blackface' minstrels' 'olio'. The shows also drew on the variety acts which toured rural America with the circuses, showboats and other kinds of troupes mentioned earlier in this chapter. With a large proportion of the American population now living close together in large cities, there was clearly less need for these different acts to travel round the countryside in order to make a living.

Two types of variety show for white people grew up towards the end of the nineteenth century. These were 'burlesque' and 'vaudeville'. Burlesque featured striptease, leg-shows and plays with a strong sexual content. As a result, burlesque attracted only male audiences. Vaudeville, on the other hand, put on entirely clean entertainment which could be attended by the whole family.

Vaudeville for white audiences was started in New York, in 1866, by Tony Pastor. At first Pastor had some difficulty persuading ladies to enter his theatre. They were used to thinking of variety theatres as undesirable places where there was a lot of smoking and drinking (ladies did not smoke in public until the

1920s), and where they were likely to see offensive and distasteful acts. However, Pastor forbade drinking and smoking, and insisted on his acts being absolutely clean. He eventually won the ladies over by offering pots, pans, dress patterns and groceries as prizes to be given away to those with winning numbers on their admission tickets. By 1881, Pastor had moved his highly successful vaudeville shows to a theatre in Union Square. He was quickly followed by other vaudeville owners, of whom the most notable was B. F. Keith.

During this time black variety theatres also grew up alongside the white. Until the early 1920s, therefore, there were two quite separate entertainment worlds in America: one for whites and one for blacks. Black artists were booked into their theatres by the Theater Owners' Booking Agency, or TOBA. Black artists did not always receive very much pay. They consequently said that the agency was Tough On Black Artists. Some, less reverently, said it was Tough On Black Asses.

It was the white *vaudeville* theatres which provided Tin Pan Alley with the best outlet for its songs. As we have seen, Tin Pan Alley made its money at this time by selling sheet music, and this sheet music was played mainly by white middle-class ladies. The only theatres into which these ladies would go to hear new songs were the vaudeville theatres.

By the early 1890s, the scene was set for the mass production and plugging of songs described in the last chapter. It was this mass production and plugging which set Tin Pan Alley publishers apart from their mid-nineteenth-century cousins. The methods of Tin Pan Alley in fact reflected the methods of the new industrial city: 'find out what the public wants and sell it to them as hard as possible.'

3 The growth of ragtime

The birth of ragtime

Right from the beginning, commercial song-writers have been quick to use different kinds of music if they think they can make money out of them. These kinds of music have frequently been Afro-American, and the first of them was ragtime. The word 'ragtime' was not in general use before 1897, when it was made famous by a Chicago newspaperman. Yet the music known as 'ragtime' existed long before 1897, and was often referred to as 'jig bands' or 'jig piano', depending on how it was played. It grew out of the jig music of black plantation slaves.

When the slaves received their freedom in 1865, many stayed and worked on the plantations. Others exercised their new-found freedom and travelled to the growing towns for work, either by river or on the railroad. In general, work was hard to come by. However, many blacks found they could earn money on the railroad itself, or in the stores, restaurants, saloons, hotels and barber shops that were growing up in the southern towns and cities. Some even came to own their own businesses and become rich. And others found they could make a living simply by playing the dance music which they had brought with them from the country.

Some of the black musicians who came to the towns of the Mississippi plains were hired by travelling minstrel shows. Many of these eventually went on to appear on the stages of the black variety theatres that were to grow up in the northern cities. Others played their music either in honky tonks (saloon bars) or bordellos (brothels). In the early pioneering days of the southern towns, honky tonks and bordellos could have been found anywhere. But as the towns became more organised and more respectable, they were restricted to small 'black' areas known as 'sporting belts' or 'Districts'. It was to these sporting belts that men, both black and white, would go to drink, play pool, gamble, pick up prostitutes and listen to music. In the end, respectable white citizens managed to get the Districts shut down. The last, New Orleans's famous Storyville, was closed in 1919.

Ragtime rhythm

The blacks who earnt a living playing music in the sporting belts of the Mississippi plains no longer had to rely on the banjo or the fiddle. With the move to the cities they gained access to the piano, and it was at this point that ragtime as we know it today began to take shape.

It is the rhythms of piano ragtime which set it apart from other kinds of music, whether Afro-American or European. The left hand of piano ragtime plays in a very regular, 'four-square' rhythm typical of European music. The right hand, however, plays in what is known as a 'syncopated' fashion. This can be heard very clearly in the opening tune of Scott Joplin's famous piano rag, 'The Entertainer'. The notes of the right hand (the melody) seem to 'cut across' those of the left hand (the bass line), and it is this 'cutting across' which makes ragtime tunes seem so catchy.

The two different rhythms of ragtime also give rise to a peculiar tug-of-war, the straight, four-square rhythms of the bass line always seeming to hold back the forward movement of the syncopated melody. It is this tug-of-war which really sets piano ragtime aside from other kinds of music.

Syncopation is, in fact, to be found in classical European music. But it only happens a few bars at a time, and there is none of the *continual* rhythmic conflict so typical of piano ragtime.

The rhythms of the right hand are African in origin. However, the remaining features of piano ragtime are all European. In particular, the melodies and harmonies have a strong European flavour. For an extreme example listen to Scott Joplin's 'Gladiolus Rag'. Apart from the syncopations, the melodies are strongly reminiscent of nineteenth-century sentimental ballads, and some of the harmonies could have come straight out of a classical symphony.

The form of piano ragtime is also very European. A blues number or a piece of jazz usually has only one melody which is constantly repeated. On each repetition the singer or instrumentalist will vary or change the melody as he goes along; this is known as 'improvisation'. A piano ragtime piece is, however, made up of three or four different sections, each one having its own tune, and there is little or no improvisation.

Ragtime goes white By the 1880s there was a large community of black ragtime pianists ('professors' or 'ticklers' as they were called), playing in the different sporting belts of the Mississippi plains. But these professors did not always stay in one town. They were frequently on the move from one District to another, picking up different ragtime melodies which they would then pass on to their friends. New tunes were learnt by ear (few professors could read or write music), and there was little feeling that these tunes were the work or property of any one player. Professors of any standing had their own styles of playing, and it was this, rather than the origin of individual tunes, which was important.

Things had to change a great deal before ragtime could be sold as sheet music by Tin Pan Alley. It had to become popular with a large number of white people because, though there were millions of black people in the USA, the large majority (about 87 per cent) was white. Unless this happened, Tin Pan Alley would not be able to make any money. Ragtime also had to be written down (the writing down of music is known as 'notation') – otherwise there could be no sheet music. Finally, the ragtime sold by Tin Pan Alley had to be easy enough to be played by amateur white pianists. It was no good trying to sell sheet music which was so difficult it could only be played by talented professional players. In the course of becoming popular with a large number of white people ragtime was to undergo many changes.

The 'blackface' minstrel shows described in the previous chapter had prepared the way for white acceptance of ragtime. Yet, as we have seen, the 'black' music played in these shows was usually only an imitation of the real thing. Ragtime proper was probably only first heard by white men when they visited the honky tonks and bordellos of the black sporting belts. But because of the purpose of their visits, these men were hardly likely to spread the word about rag music to the rest of polite white society. It should be remembered that most of America's amateur pianists were women, and until ragtime was made acceptable to them, it would not become a Tin Pan Alley success. Ragtime needed to find its way into vaudeville.

The man who put it there was Ben Harney. On 17 February 1896, a New York theatre paper (the *New York Clipper*) reported that 'Ben R. Harney, another stranger . . . jumped into immediate favor through the medium of his genuinely clever plantation Negro imitations and excellent piano playing.' Harney, who was white, had been born in the State of Kentucky, in 1871. Like any other white man living in the area at this time, he would have been able to hear the music of black people. But, at the age of seventeen, Harney became really fascinated by it. Not long afterwards he was to be found playing the piano in bars and dance halls in Louisville. Harney and his wife also spent a number of years on the road with black artists working as travelling entertainers.

When he came to New York in the mid-1890s, Harney had completely soaked up the world of black music and entertainment, and was one of the very few whites who could play black music as well as the blacks themselves. His success at Keith's Theater and Tony Pastor's Theater in New York's Union Square guaranteed the future popularity of ragtime with white audiences. But the word 'ragtime' was not in common use in 1896. A variety of terms such as 'jig piano', 'jig bands' and 'rags' were used. What was needed was one common label which would fire the imagination of white audiences across the country.

The word 'ragtime' became fashionable not as a direct result of Harney's New York breakthrough, but as a result of the growing popularity of the Cakewalk with white people. Roy Carew, a ragtime enthusiast, recounts the way in which minstrel shows spread this dance across the country:

People would see the cakewalk performed and come home and learn how to do it. Road shows and minstrels carried it to small places everywhere . . . Just before 1897 there was a huge cakewalk craze and every hamlet in the country had contests.

Not surprisingly, the imitation jig music to which it was danced also became popular. In 1897, an unknown Chicago journalist first put the term 'ragtime' into print to describe this music. In doing so, he unknowingly gave birth to Tin Pan Alley's first big fad.

However, Tin Pan Alley could not take advantage of the ragtime–cakewalk craze without sheet music, and for this they needed ragtime in a written form. As one publisher put it: 'White or colored folk didn't even know how to write ragtime syncopation. A system had to be worked out before ragtime got to be published.'

The major figure in the history of notated ragtime was Scott Joplin. He was probably the first person successfully to capture genuine ragtime rhythms on paper, and it is mainly because of him that classic ragtime as we know it today has survived. However, Scott Joplin was a black man, and it was much more difficult for blacks to get music published than it was for whites. So it was white man Ben Harney who first got a ragtime piece published, in 1895. This piece was 'You've Been a Good Old Wagon but You've Done Broke Down'.

The title of the song does not of course refer to 'ragtime'. But as soon as the word became fashionable, in 1897, the aim of song-writers was to get pieces published with the magic word 'ragtime' (or 'rag') on the cover – not necessarily to write genuine ragtime.

Yet another change had to take place if a form of ragtime was to be accepted by white people. This was in the speed, or *tempo*, at which the music was played. As we have seen, the particular appeal of piano ragtime depends on the conflict of rhythms between the melody line and the bass line. But this conflict will only give rise to ragtime's catchy and lilting quality if the music is not played too fast. The bass line must be played steadily if it is successfully to hold back the syncopated forward movement of the melody.

This secret of playing ragtime was completely lost on the many white pianists who wanted to cash in on Harney's success. Their aim was to grab the audience's attention – not necessarily to reproduce faithfully black ragtime music. And, generally speaking, the more brilliant and flashy the music, the more the audience liked it. So after 1897 the word 'ragtime' was used to describe any music played in a fast, 'syncopated' manner. The most successful of Harney's imitators was Mike Bernard (dubbed 'Rag Time King of the World'). Not long after Harney's first New York appearance Bernard appeared playing a piece called 'Fantasy on the Pilgrim's Chorus from Tanhauser and the Finale to Rubinstein's E flat Concerto'. This was not ragtime. It was sheer showmanship.

Because of the changes which have been described above, two kinds of ragtime existed side by side from 1897 onwards. There was the genuine black ragtime which was developed into a restrained and polished type of music by Scott Joplin. And there was the flashy, brilliant, fast music to which Tin Pan Alley gave the name 'ragtime'. The Tin Pan Alley variety remained very popular until about 1909, when the fashion began to die down a bit. However, the year 1911 saw the publication of the most famous of Tin Pan Alley 'ragtime' tunes, Irving Berlin's 'Alexander's Ragtime Band'. This revived ragtime and it lived on until about 1917, when the second big Tin Pan Alley fashion, jazz, began to take over.

The difference between genuine ragtime and the commercial variety can easily be heard by listening to Scott Joplin's 'The Entertainer' and then Irving Berlin's 'Alexander's Ragtime Band'. 'The Entertainer' is played at a measured pace, the melodies are highly syncopated, and there is a rhythmic conflict between the right and left hands. Finally, the piece has four main sections, each with its own melody. 'Alexander's Ragtime Band' is played much faster. There is only one melody, which is quite catchy but not syncopated. There is also no rhythmic conflict between the melody and the bass line. Syncopation and rhythmic conflict were in fact the last things that Tin Pan Alley wanted in its ragtime. They made the music very hard to play, and thus of little appeal to amateur white pianists.

Scott Joplin and John Stark   Scott Joplin was born in Texarkana, Texas, in 1868. He showed an early interest in a neighbour's piano, and news of his ability as a player reached the ears of white people through the talk of black servants. As a result, an old German music teacher began to give the young boy lessons on the piano, and, perhaps even more important, on how to write harmony. So at a very early age Joplin had a knowledge both of the music of his own people, and of the European music of the whites.

His knowledge of black music deepened while touring the sporting belts of the Mississippi plains as a pianist. However, on arriving at the Missouri town of Sedalia, in 1896, Joplin once again took up his study of harmony, this time at the George Smith College for Negroes. And instead of contenting himself just making money in the town's sporting belt, he set himself the task of composing and writing down piano ragtime pieces. It was Joplin's aim to see ragtime become accepted, alongside the classical European music he was studying, as a serious art-form. This means that he wanted people to listen to it attentively in concert halls and theatres, and not just see it as purely commercial light entertainment or background music.

He was helped in this aim by John Stark, the white owner of a Sedalia music shop. It was Stark who, in September 1899, published Joplin's 'Maple Leaf Rag'. 'Maple Leaf Rag' was not in fact the first Joplin rag to be published. 'Original Rags' had already been published in March of the same year by Carl Hoffman of Kansas. But 'Maple Leaf Rag' sold in great numbers, and quickly made Joplin famous.

The money from 'Maple Leaf Rag' allowed Joplin to give up playing in the sporting belts and work entirely on writing new pieces. It also gave Stark the chance to move to the more important city of St Louis and start up as a full-time publisher. This he did in 1900. Encouraged by his successes, Stark moved on to New York in 1905. But here he came up against the publishers of Tin Pan Alley ragtime, and the classic ragtime which he was determined to sell did not do very well.

opposite
'The Entertainer', a Scott Joplin tune, published by John Stark, and subsequently made famous through the movie *The Sting*, starring Paul Newman and Robert Redford

Joplin followed Stark to St Louis in 1900 and then to New York in 1907, but his friendship with the publisher was becoming strained. This was mainly because of the composer's wish to write and publish a full-length opera. Stark had already lost money publishing Joplin's *The Rag Time Dance* (1906), a

twenty-minute stage presentation needing a small
orchestra, a narrator, and a company of dancers. So
he was hardly encouraged to publish the opera,

Treemonisha. In its piano version alone it ran to 230 pages!

In 1908 Joplin broke with Stark, and after that his piano pieces were published by the Seminary Music Company of New York. It was from the extra money he made with this company that Joplin himself published *Treemonisha* in 1911. The only performance was in Harlem, in 1915, and again this had to be financed by Joplin himself. The performance was not a success, and Joplin's dreams of seeing ragtime become an art-form alongside classical European music were dashed. He died two years later in 1917, the year that jazz replaced ragtime as the big Tin Pan Alley fashion.

But although ragtime never became an art-form in the same way as classical European music, Joplin did succeed in leaving behind him a music that was restrained and polished. In this, the music was different from the rags of the professors, which were usually faster and livelier. But Joplin's music still contained the rhythmic conflict already described, and was played at a slower speed than Tin Pan Alley ragtime.

Opposition to ragtime

By 1900, both Tin Pan Alley ragtime and Scott Joplin had made their mark. Yet it should not be imagined that ragtime, whether white or black, was accepted by all white Americans. In 1901, for example, we find *Metronome* magazine assuring white Americans that 'ragtime's days are numbered. We are sorry to think that anyone should imagine that ragtime was of the least musical importance. It was a popular wave in the wrong direction.'

Far from being 'a popular wave in the wrong direction', ragtime was to give birth to jazz. But why did some white Americans oppose ragtime? There are two main reasons. First, ragtime had been the music of a despised race, the blacks, and had grown out of the Districts which respectable white citizens were keen to shut down. Ragtime 'exalts noise, rush and street vulgarity,' complained *Musical America* in 1913. 'It suggests repulsive dance-halls and restaurants.'

Second, ragtime was seen as a threat to classical European music. In 1901, the president of the American Federation of Musicians ordered his members to stop playing ragtime. 'The musicians know what is good,' he said, 'and if people don't we will have to teach them.' In order to put down ragtime, classical musicians tried to show that it was not as good as their kind of music. The *Musician* of November 1901, for instance, asserted that 'unusual rhythmic combinations and syncopations have been so extensively used by high-class composers that it is not possible for coon song composers to invent anything along these lines.'

But, as we saw earlier, syncopations of ragtime *were* different from those used in classical European music. So, in trying to put down ragtime, the *Musician* had simply shown that it did not fully understand this kind of music. Mistakes of this sort were to be repeated many times in the years that followed.

4 The ragtime era

Dance craze During the first ten years of this century, there were basically two kinds of dancing in America. At one extreme, there were dances such as the waltz which had been brought over from Europe during the eighteenth and nineteenth centuries. They were rather stiff and formal, and were performed at polite society balls by wealthy white Americans. The balls were usually private affairs, and the music was provided by refined string orchestras. At the other end of the social scale were the 'animal' dances performed by blacks and some whites in the public dance halls of cities. Middle-class white Americans thought of these dance halls in much the same way as they thought of early variety theatres. They were undesirable and distasteful places not fit to be frequented by respectable white families. The animal dances performed there grew out of older plantation dances such as the Cakewalk. They differed greatly from the European dances of polite society balls.

The European dances had three important features. First of all, they had a strict and intricate set of steps which were difficult to perform correctly. Second, all bodily movement in these dances grew upwards from the movement of the feet. Finally, the music was written for the dances, rather than the dances growing out of the music.

The animal dances that developed from the Cakewalk worked in a completely different way, however. The different dances were created in response to ragtime music. As famous society dancer Vernon Castle put it: 'The waltz is beautiful, the tango is graceful, the Brazilian maxixe is unique. One can sit quietly and listen with pleasure to them all; but when a good orchestra plays a "rag" one has simply *got* to move.' Individual ragtime steps were easy to do and not so important as the steps of European dances. Finally, individual dancers were allowed a great deal of freedom in their movements, which began from the hips and not from the feet.

The new American dances were called animal dances because they imitated the movements of animals. Dancers did the Funky Butt, the Buzzard Lope, the Turkey Trot, the Bunny Hug, the Grizzly Bear, the Monkey Glide and the Kangaroo Dip. They also walked the dog and balled the jack. Some even invented steps right on the dance floor.

The era of ragtime music and ragtime dance was an exciting and breathtaking one. There was a feeling of change in the air, and this was reflected not only in the greater freedom of the new dances but also in the way that women took part in them. The older European dances came from a society that had strict morals. This accounted for their strict and formal movements, as well as for the fact that couples were not allowed to hold each other too closely. The European dances also came from a society in which men were much more important than women. As a result, it was the men who led the women in these dances. The men decided which steps were going to be danced as well as the direction the couple were going to take round the dance floor.

With the new American dances the freer body movements reflected a greater sexual freedom. Couples walked and trotted round the dance floor in a rocking, swooping manner, swaying outwards with each step. And, as names like the Grizzly Bear and the Bunny Hug suggest, couples held each other very closely indeed. The Bunny Hug was considered so indecent it was banned for a few years. Also, women were as free as men to do the steps they wanted. It is said, for example, that a New Jersey girl ended up in prison because she put a leg-split in her Turkey Trot! Women were gradually to take over the dance floor. By the time jazz was established in the early 1920s, they were doing Shimmy solos while men simply looked on in admiration.

In the years before 1911, the Cakewalk and animal dances started creeping into polite society balls. The Cakewalk in fact quickly became the rage right across America and Europe. But the growing freedom and greater sexual appeal of these dances did not meet with total approval from white middle-class Americans. The dances were considered too crude and distasteful for polite white society, and as a result they were changed into something more refined. The Turkey Trot, for example, became the One-step. There was no longer to be any rocking, swaying or trotting. The ease of the animal dances was to be linked to the elegance of European dances:

opposite
The Bunny Hug
Ban: Miss Bee
Thompson
wearing a
bumper to defeat
the ban (June
1923)

Bear in mind this one important point: when I say walk, that is all it is. Do not shuffle, do not bob up and down or trot. Simply walk as softly and as smoothly as possible, taking a step to every count of the music . . . It is simply one step – hence its name.

These instructions come from a book called *Modern Dancing* which was written in 1914 by Irene and Vernon Castle. The Castles were by far the most famous dancing team of the time, and were responsible for encouraging modern ballroom dancing as a public pastime for middle-class Americans. The dance with which they had the most success was the Foxtrot. This, too, grew out of the animal dances, and was, until 1914, also known as the Horse Trot or the Fish Walk. In the autumn of 1914 it really took off, and the future of the American dance craze was assured.

What gave rise to the American dance craze? First, ragtime music had been accepted by many white Americans as early as 1897. The popularity of the Cakewalk had quite a lot to do with this acceptance, and it seems likely that many white Americans had been doing the Cakewalk in the privacy of their own homes since at least the turn of the century. It was only a matter of time before the Cakewalk was danced in public by respectable white Americans, and new *American* dances developed from it. Second, the Cakewalk, the animal dances, and the more polite dances that grew out of them were much easier to perform than the European dances. They were more spontaneous, and did not require hours of painstaking practice or coaching by a dance instructor. Finally, it was much more fun and much easier to dance the One-step or the Foxtrot than it was to stay at home and sing and play sheet music.

The new dance craze that spread across America after 1911 was thus another step away from entertaining oneself at home. In chapter 2 we saw how the mainly rural population of mid-nineteenth-century America entertained themselves with song.

opposite
The supremely elegant Irene Castle

THE CAKE WALK AS PRACTISED IN ITS NATIVE HOME

The Cake Walk, which has become the rage in Paris, came originally from the Southern States of America, where it flourished about fifty years ago. The negroes copied the walk from the Indians, and gradually developed it until at length prizes were offered for the most accomplished performer. Later the name "Cake Walk" was adopted because the prize was usually a big cake. At these competitions the negroes used to turn out in their best array. From the Southern States the dance went further north, and has now found its way to Europe. In Paris the "Cak Yak," as it is called in France, first made its appearance at the music halls, and now is popular in the drawing room.

THE CAKE WALK AS ADAPTED TO THE PARIS DRAWING ROOM
DRAWN BY GEORGES SCOTT

The original Cakewalk and its white ballroom successor. Notice how the blacks in the top picture seem to be enjoying themselves so much, and how restrained and foppish the dance has become in the second

They were only occasionally visited by troupes of travelling entertainers. With the quick increase in the urban population and the growth of permanent variety theatres, there was less need for people to entertain themselves. But with the new dance craze *respectable* white dance halls sprang up right across the country: turkey trotting, bunny hugging, smoking and the wearing of hats indoors were forbidden. These new dance halls provided middle-class Americans with an excellent opportunity of getting out of the house. Not only were the dances fun, but dance halls were places where people could meet and get to know one another. The hearth of the rural homestead had been replaced by the bubble and excitement of the city dance hall. Dancing became so important to white Americans between 1911 and 1915 that restaurants had to have dance floors to attract customers and make any money. Again, hotels of any standing quickly equipped themselves with ballrooms.

The American dance craze gave rise to a new kind of dance band. In the days of polite society balls, the music was provided by string orchestras. Since most of the balls were private affairs, very few of the orchestras were full-time. As often as not they were put together at the last moment, and were made up of classically trained musicians who wanted to earn some extra money. But with the growth of respectable dance halls, restaurant dance floors and hotel ballrooms, the need arose for a considerable number of full-time groups who could provide music day after day. However, string orchestras and the musicians who played in them were of little use for this kind of work. For one thing, string orchestras produced a smooth and soft, sweet-sounding music that had little in common with the peppy new American dances. Also, the syncopation of ragtime music was difficult to perform. Some string orchestra musicians found they could not play it. Others just refused to.

As a result, a new kind of band came into being around 1911. One of the first of these was organised by James Reese Europe, a black American from Mobile, Alabama. Shortly after 1914, Europe's band was hired by the Castles for a dancing demonstration they were giving in Philadelphia. Following this, Europe became the Castle's musical director, and he and his eighteen-piece, all-black band toured with the famous dancing couple all over America. They also helped put on the highly successful 'Castles in the Air' show on a hotel roof-top in New York.

The early dance bands were not usually as big as Europe's, however. Art Hickman, for example, had a ten-piece band made up of a cornet, a trombone, two saxophones, a piano, two banjos, drums, a violin and a double bass. But even that was considered large for the time. Most early dance bands quickly settled down to having just two brass instruments, two saxophones and a rhythm section made up of a piano, a banjo and drums. Sometimes, a brass bass or a tuba was added. Hickman's band (which started life in San Francisco in 1913), was unusual in having a string bass. These did not become a regular feature of dance bands or jazz bands until the early 1930s. Hickman was also the first dance band leader to make saxophones such an important part of his line-up. With their loud wind instruments and strong rhythm sections these bands were much more suited to ragtime dancing than the softly spoken string orchestras.

opposite
An advert for Jim Europe and his band on their triumphant return from the First World War

LIEUT. "JIM"

EUROPE (HIM-SELF)

AND HIS FAMOUS

369th U. S. INFANTRY

JAZZ BAND

DIRECT FROM THE FIGHTING FRONTS IN FRANCE

The Band That
Played the

Hell Fighters

On To
Victory

At the Battles of Champagne and Argonne Forest!

The Band
That Set All
France

JAZZ
MAD!

65

BATTLING
MUSICIANS

THE BAND MARCHING THROUGH PARIS

Before the
War New
York's Most
Popular
Dance Band

65

Masters
Of JAZZ!

Hear
Them Go

OVER THE TOP!

Of The
Musical Trenches

HEAR

The Famous Singing Serenaders
The World's Greatest Saxaphone Septette
The Soul Stirring Negro Spirituals
The Moaning Trombone—in the "Blues"
The Bombardment of the Percussion Twins

Alexander takes his ragtime band to France

In 1917 America entered the First World War on the side of the Allies (Britain, France, Belgium, Italy and Russia) against the Central Powers (Germany, Austria and Hungary). Plain Jim Europe became Lieutenant James Europe. He formed the highly talented all-black 369th Infantry ('Hell Fighters') Band, and took it across the Atlantic to entertain the troops. The band was a huge success and did much to popularise American ragtime music in France. On its return to New York at the end of the war the band marched down Fifth Avenue to a hero's welcome. However, not long afterwards Europe was dead. On 9 May 1919 he had a fierce argument with one of his drummers, Herbert Wright. Wright stabbed Europe and the bandleader died from his wounds a few hours later.

The war was also important for the Tin Pan Alley writers who had stayed behind in America. Many of these writers were Jewish immigrants who had come from Eastern and Central Europe. Some 20 million immigrants entered America between 1880 and 1910, and most of them went to live in the cities. This in part explains the fast growth of city populations described in chapter 2. However, these immigrants were not easily accepted by native-born white Americans, many of whose ancestors came from Britain or Ireland. The immigrants spoke languages other than English. They were looked on with suspicion and thought of as second-class citizens. Above all, they found it very difficult to enter respectable professions such as law, banking and medicine.

As a result, many immigrants (as well as the American-born children of immigrants) went into the rather less desirable entertainment business. There was, as we have seen, a lot of money to be made in this business, and many immigrants were very successful at it. However, not even a rich immigrant could expect easy acceptance from Anglo-Saxon Americans, and it was this acceptance which the immigrants were above all else keen to have. They were anxious to become 'good Americans'. For this reason they changed their traditional ways and even their names.

The First World War provided the immigrants of Tin Pan Alley with a tremendous opportunity to show what good Americans they were. Music has always played an important part in wars. It spurs on armies and keeps up the morale of ordinary people. The First World War was no exception in giving rise to music, and it was not of course difficult for Tin Pan Alley to come up with patriotic songs. But the Alley had one further great advantage. For twenty years it had been in the business of persuading Americans to buy its songs in very large numbers. If any organisation knew how to get an idea across to the American people, and how to get them enthusiastic about it, it was Tin Pan Alley.

The American government wanted to get the American people behind the war. Tin Pan Alley had the best publicity machine in the country and wanted to become respectable. The result was a flood of songs about the war. 'Hello, Central, Give Me Heaven' became 'Hello, Central, Give Me No Man's Land'. A mother boasted that 'They Were All Out of Step but Jim', while a girlfriend was of the opinion that 'If He Can Fight Like He Can Love, Goodnight Germany'. Sometimes the Alley tried too hard, and came up with puns like 'Your Lips Are No Man's Land but Mine'. Even 'Alexander's Ragtime Band' was pressed into service in 'When Alexander Takes His Band to France'.

An outstanding example of the immigrant song-writer is Irving Berlin. He was born in 1888, in the small Russian town of Temun, and his original name was Israel Baline. In line with many other immigrant song-writers he later changed it for something more American-sounding. In 1890, the Balines moved to New York. Just six years later Berlin's father died. In order not to be a burden on his mother, Berlin ran away from home when only fourteen, and started to get various jobs as a singer.

After working for Harry von Tilzer as a song plugger and 'plant', Berlin started to write his own songs. He was eventually taken on as a staff lyricist by Ted Snyder, a composer and publisher. Then, because Berlin wrote so many hit songs, Snyder asked him to become a partner in his publishing business. Finally, in 1911, came 'Alexander's Ragtime Band', and, at the age of twenty-three, Berlin had become America's most successful song-writer.

Berlin was to remain a leading Tin Pan Alley writer for a great number of years. He was the composer of many songs which are still often heard today, such as 'A Pretty Girl is Like a Melody' (1919), 'Always' (1925) and 'Blue Skies' (1927). What made him unique, however, was that he also became a leading writer of American musicals. (Stage and film musicals are discussed in chapter 6. For the moment they may be thought of as plays or films which contain songs, and which sometimes have complete musical scores.) During the 1930s, Berlin wrote the music for three films starring the world-famous dancing team of Fred Astaire and Ginger Rogers. The films were *Top Hat* (1935), *Follow the Fleet* (1936), and *Carefree* (1938). The production of Berlin's greatest stage musical, *Annie Get Your Gun*,

opposite Irving Berlin in 1912, one year after the publication of 'Alexander's Ragtime Band'. Notice the comment on the photograph: 'This is the life'

came in 1946. It is this show which contains the well-known anthem of the theatre business, 'There's No Business Like Show Business'.

The main reason for Berlin's unequalled success as an Alleyman and a composer of musicals is that, more than most other song-writers, he has an uncanny understanding of the feelings of ordinary people. During the First World War, for example, he wrote 'Oh, How I Hate To Get Up in the Morning' (1918), a song which must have summed up the sentiments of many an American soldier. The song 'White Christmas' (1942), which became a big hit for Bing Crosby, is again typical in that it reflects the true atmosphere of Christmas for a great many people.

Berlin's career is a real American 'rags-to-riches' story. He started life as the son of immigrants. He was poor, and had precious little education, musical or otherwise. Yet he was to become one of a handful of extremely famous American popular composers, as well as a highly successful businessman.

Handy and the blues

There was one other type of Afro-American music to be taken over by Tin Pan Alley during the ragtime era, and that was the blues. As we have seen, the blues were one of the three main ways in which early Afro-American music developed during the nineteenth century. Like ragtime, the blues found their way into minstrel shows, where they were performed by singers such as Ma Rainey, the 'Mother of the Blues'.

It was with one of these minstrel troupes that William C. Handy, a black trumpeter, got his first regular job. He was born in Florence, Alabama, in 1873. In 1909 he wrote a song for an election campaign in Memphis. The candidate romped home.

opposite
The statue of Handy erected in his memory in Handy Park, Memphis

Encouraged by this, Handy turned the song into a piano piece, but was at first unable to find anyone to buy it. In the end, a New York publisher bought it outright. This meant that Handy received no royalties or further payments. Lyrics were added to the piece, the song was an immediate success, and the publisher made a great deal of money.

Upset by this, Handy set out to write another blues song which this time would make money for him. 'St Louis Blues', his greatest success, was completed in September 1914. Determined not to be robbed by publishers again, Handy published 'St Louis Blues' himself in association with another black man, Harry Pace. Sales were slow at first, but, in 1918, Handy and Pace moved their publishing business to New York; the song was performed by white singer Sophie Tucker in vaudeville, and sales really took off.

As a result of this success, Handy became known as the 'Father of the Blues', but it is not correct to think of him in this way. As we have seen, the blues had been around for at least fifty years before he wrote his song. Their history is described by Graham Vulliamy in *Jazz and Blues*

Because the original, rural blues sounded very rough and ready compared to the songs of Tin Pan Alley, they had to be written and performed in a way that was acceptable to white people if they were to become popular. Like ragtime, therefore, the blues needed to undergo three changes.

First, they had to be written down so that Tin Pan Alley had something to sell. Handy had now achieved this, though in Handy's notated versions the blues became very watered down indeed. This was partially because it is impossible to write down accurately the way blues music is actually performed. Musical notation was designed to be used by classical musicians using a fixed, *in-tune* scale. But blues artists make great use of 'blue notes', that is, notes which seem to classical musicians to be bent *out* of tune. Second, the blues had to be brought to white vaudeville theatres so that white people could actually hear them. This was done by white artists such as Al Jolson (see chapter 8) and Sophie Tucker, both of whom heard the blues performed by black singers in black vaudeville theatres. When the blues moved to vaudeville, however, they became much more refined. It is said that while classic blues singers *sang* the blues, the vaudeville artists merely *acted* them. Third, the rural blues also had a high sexual content. In their new form there was little or no sexual content, and the lyrics were sung more cleanly.

As a result of these changes, Handy's music ended up having as much to do with white dance music as it did with the real blues. This is something Handy himself admits in his autobiography. 'When "St. Louis Blues" was written the tango was in vogue,' he said. 'I tricked the dancers by arranging a tango introduction, breaking abruptly into a low-down blues.' Handy had turned the blues white.

The death of ragtime

The First World War may have made Tin Pan Alley respectable. But it also spelt the end of ragtime. In its efforts to become respectable Tin Pan Alley did something it had never done before, and was never to do again. It became involved in a political and moral issue. It had played a big part in persuading Americans that entering the First World War was right, and that not to support this entry was unpatriotic and wrong. The war was a very serious affair.

In the years following the First World War, the American people had a change of heart. They wanted to forget the seriousness of war and have fun. Tin Pan Alley, of course, was in business to provide that fun. But because Americans had marched to war on ragtime, and because ragtime had become associated with the seriousness of war, it could no longer be part of that fun. Ragtime had in fact been in decline when America entered the war in 1917. By the end of 1918 it sounded tired and old-fashioned. The American people needed something new, and that something was jazz.

5 The jazz age

Jazz The development of jazz is described by Graham
Vulliamy in *Jazz and Blues*. For the moment it is
sufficient to say that the music we are talking about
was like that played by the late Louis Armstrong or
like the 'trad jazz' of present-day bands such as
Chris Barber's.

The main difference between ragtime and jazz is that
whereas ragtime was black city music played on the
piano, jazz was black city music played by bands.
These bands had two sections which were similar to
the two hands of piano ragtime. The melody section
– usually made up of a cornet (a kind of trumpet),
clarinet and trombone – was the 'right hand' of the
jazz band, while the 'left hand', or rhythm section,
was made up from instruments such as the drums,
piano, banjo, tuba or string bass, and guitar.
    The change from pianos to bands resulted in a
change in the music. Jazz did not have the rhythmic
tug-of-war typical of ragtime. Instead, all the
instruments created their own syncopated lines.
When combined, the total effect of these was a new
type of rhythmic feel known as 'swing'. Because of
its three or more melodic instruments, jazz also had
more than one melody at a time, some of which were
made up by the musicians as they went along. This

improvisation, as it was known, as well as the
numerous melodies and swing, quickly made jazz
the newest and most exciting form of black
American music. However, like ragtime and the
blues, jazz was taken over by many white
Americans for their own entertainment.

The band who first made jazz popular with white
Americans was the Original Dixieland Jazz Band
(ODJB). The band was made up of five white
musicians who came from New Orleans. It was there
that they heard a great deal of the music played by
early black jazz bands. Nick LaRocca, the cornettist
and driving force behind the band, spent many hours
getting his musicians to play in a proper jazz style.
Gradually this style came into being. LaRocca would
provide the melody, Larry Shields (the clarinettist)
would improvise round it in a kind of running,
'noodling' style, Eddie Edwards (the trombonist)
would add harmony and rhythm, while Henry Ragas
(piano) and Tony Sbarbaro (drums) would keep the
music swinging along. LaRocca was especially proud
of the way the three melodic instruments would 'talk'
to each other as if they were having a conversation.
'It's like a dress,' said LaRocca. 'I cut the material,
Shields puts on the lace, and Edwards sews it up.'

It was in January 1917 that the band moved to
New York and made its famous appearance at
Reisenweber's restaurant. The paper *Variety*
described the tremendous success of this band.

> The genuine 'jazz' band at Reisenweber's . . .
> appears to be drawing business there. Late in the
> morning the jazzers go to work and the dancers
> hit the floor, to remain there until they topple over,
> if the band keeps on playing. It leaves no question
> but that they like to dance to that kind of music.

The Original Dixieland Jazz Band. As this photograph shows, part of their appeal was the way they acted the fool on stage

Jazz gave rise to new dances. The best-known of these was the Shimmy, made famous by Frank Hale and Signe Patterson in a vaudeville act at Keith's Colonial Theater in 1917. The Shimmy was performed by standing with toes together, heels apart, and swivelling the shoulders. Compared even to the One-step, Foxtrot or animal dances, the Shimmy was a very daring dance, especially for women. In 1920, the ODJB was joined by a solo dancer, Gilda Gray. Her appearance on the dance floor in a bright red dress decorated with spangles caused a sensation. When asked by a customer what she was doing, she replied, 'I'm shaking my shimmy, that's what I'm doing.' Gilda Gray was a symbol of women's increasing freedom in society. It was not long before they would be smoking in public!

The ODJB made black jazz understandable for white audiences by keeping melodies recognisable. However, as time went on, white audiences demanded a smoother and more refined sound for their dancing. The first band leader to cash in on this demand was Paul Whiteman.

> We first met – jazz and I – at a dance hall dive . . . It screeched and bellowed at me from a trick platform in the middle of a smoke-hazed, beer-fumed room. And it hit me hard. Raucous? Yes. Crude – undoubtedly. Unmusical – sure as you live. But rhythmic, catching as the smallpox and spirit-lifting.

These were the words with which white bandleader Paul Whiteman described his first encounter with jazz. His reaction was not untypical of many white Americans. But unlike those white people who, as we shall see, tried to stamp out jazz, Whiteman realised that there was money to be made by turning jazz into a dance music acceptable to polite white society.

Whiteman had his first big success in 1920, when he and his band appeared at the Palais Royal Cafe in New York. Whiteman's audience at this time included such prominent American families as the Vanderbilts, not to mention members of the English artistocracy such as Lord and Lady Mountbatten. With important people like these dancing to his music, Whiteman quickly became *the* showbusiness personality of the age. He became known as the 'King of Jazz', and he and his band remained popular into the 1930s.

With its increasing success, the Whiteman organisation gradually changed from a dance band into a show band. The most important moment in this change came in 1924 when the twenty-three-piece band gave a 'symphonic' concert in New York's

Aeolian Hall. There was no dancing on this occasion. The audience sat and listened to a programme of music which climaxed with George Gershwin's especially composed *Rhapsody in Blue* for piano and orchestra. George Gershwin's importance to the history of popular music is described in chapter 6.

Whiteman's attempt to turn jazz into an art-form alongside European classical music was similar to Scott Joplin's attempt to turn ragtime into an art-form. Like Joplin, Whiteman had received a training in classical music. But, unlike Joplin, who was thoroughly steeped in ragtime, Whiteman had little real understanding of the Afro-American music he was attempting to make respectable. He was no more the 'King of Jazz' than Handy was the 'Father of the Blues' or Mike Bernard the 'Rag Time King of the World'.

What was it that made Whiteman's music different from that of the ODJB? For a start it sounded sweeter. Whiteman added flutes, strings and, above all, saxophones to smooth down the robust sound of cornets, clarinets and trombones. The music also had little swing.

But the most important difference between Whiteman's music and that of the ODJB lay in the way it was created. The ODJB's numbers were put together by ear, and each performance was different because of the improvisation that took place between the three melodic instruments. Whiteman's music, on the other hand, was written down, and the final sound was the work of a professional arranger. This use of notation prevented improvisation. Each player had to play exactly the same notes in each performance, and any individual musical expression was forbidden. Indeed, the souvenir programme for a Whiteman tour of 1925–6 explained that the bandleader 'confined his repertoire to pieces which were scored and forbade his players to depart from the script.'

Instructions such as this made life difficult for the genuine jazz musicians that Whiteman employed after 1927. The legendary Bix Beiderbecke, for example, was not good at reading music, and had difficulty in mastering the parts he was supposed to play. (Bix Beiderbecke is discussed by Graham Vulliamy in *Jazz and Blues*.) The difference between improvised jazz and notated dance band music was so great that some jazz musicians were afraid to learn to read music in case they would no longer be able to play jazz. 'It's like this,' New Orleans clarinettist Gus Mueller explained to Paul Whitemen one day. 'I knew a boy once down in N'Awleens that was a hot player, but he learned to read music and then he couldn't play jazz any more. I don't want to be like that.' Mueller eventually resigned from the Whiteman band. Pressed for a reason he exclaimed: 'Nuh, suh, I jes' can't play that "pretty music" that you all play. And you fellers can't never play blues worth a damn.'

When he died, in 1967, Whiteman was described as the 'King of the Jazz Age'. This was a much more accurate description than the 'King of Jazz'. For although Whiteman's music had little to do with jazz, his activities as a showman and entertainer were typical of the era. He was an imposing figure, weighing over twenty stones (280 lbs) and always dressing immaculately. He and his organisation lived and travelled in luxury (Cadillacs were the order of the day), and it was common knowledge that his musicians were the highest paid in the business. Paul Whiteman was very much larger than life.

Paul Whiteman and his Orchestra. This band is clearly much more polite and formal than the Original Dixieland Jazz Band

Like 'ragtime', 'jazz' was just as much a label as it was a kind of music. It not only described a music, but a new attitude to life which swept many white Americans off their feet in a way that could not have been dreamt of before the First World War. The war gave many Americans their first taste of European life, and when these soldiers returned home they found their previous lives, including good old ragtime, very dull. The words of one topical song sum up the feelings:

Every time he looks at me
He makes me feel so unnecessary
Oh! Just think of it Clarice,
He spent two months in Paris, and
Oh! Oh! Johnny's in town!!

As Paul Whiteman said: 'The time was right to almost any explosion.' Jazz was 'the expression of the soul of America and America recognizes it.'

But not all Americans recognised it. As with ragtime, jazz came in for a lot of criticism. And, as with ragtime, there were two main reasons for it.

First, jazz had strong links with America's black population. In many cases, it had grown out of the Districts or sporting belts described in chapter 3. As white jazz clarinettist Milton Mezzrow wrote, 'our music was called "nigger music" and "whorehouse music" and "nice" people turned up their noses at it.' Jazz was seen as especially dangerous because, unlike ragtime, it seemed to run through every aspect of American life. This fear was expressed in the *New York Times*, in 1926, by a Baptist clergyman.

> I have no patience with this modern jazz tendency, whether it be in music, science, social life or religion. It is part of the lawless spirit which is being manifested in many departments of life, endangering our civilization in its general revolt against authority and established order.

Second, jazz was seen as a very great threat to classical European music. Never before had white Americans been so gripped by a new form of popular music. Reactions were strong. One journalist wrote that jazz had a 'blah! blah!' that reminded him of 'the way that live sheep are turned into mutton.' A Princeton University professor went so far as to say that jazz 'is not music at all.'

In general, it was only the youth of America who recognised that jazz was 'the expression of the soul of America'. Older people thought otherwise, and it was they who had power and money. Gradually, older Americans did away with what they thought of as the worst aspects of the jazz age. In 1920, the Prohibition Laws made the drinking of alcohol illegal, and in 1922 all jazz and dancing was forbidden after midnight on New York's Broadway. By the mid-1920s the type of jazz played by the ODJB was becoming a memory. All that remained was the smoother, politer dance music of the Paul Whiteman variety.

Records and radio Jazz had been made popular by the ODJB, and its place in the history of white American popular music established by Paul Whiteman. But the spread of jazz had also been greatly helped through the making of records.

The phonograph, as the record player was first called, was invented by Thomas Edison in 1877. Until 1925, all recordings were made mechanically and *not* electronically, as is the case today. The sound was collected through a big tin horn, at the end of which was placed a metal needle. The vibrations of the sound made the needle move up and down on a rotating wax cylinder, thus cutting a groove. At first, the quality of the sound recorded in this way was not very good, but it improved when the cylinder was replaced by the flat disc.

The first recordings of music were made around 1894. To begin with, the record companies (notably the Columbia Gramophone Company and the Victor Talking Machine Company) recorded only classical music. But by the early years of this century the companies realised that much more money was to be made recording popular music. Sales increased greatly during the dance craze that began in 1911, and by 1914 the recording industry was firmly established.

The great advantage of records, of course, was that they could be heard in the privacy of people's homes. No longer was it necessary to go to a vaudeville theatre or a dance hall to hear a favourite band. Dancing to jazz music could now become a private affair. But records were especially helpful in

A3716

NEW AND NOVEL

AN ENTERTAINMENT which presents the newest and most wonderful Musical Instrument and Talking Machine known to the present century

THE GRAPHOPHONE GRAND

This wonderful instrument must not for a moment be compared to the ordinary Talking Machines which have been heard through the country for years.

The Graphophone Grand
ACTUALLY ACCOMPLISHES
WHAT HAS HITHERTO BEEN DEEMED
THE IMPOSSIBLE.

PERFECTLY REPRODUCES THE HUMAN VOICE
JUST AS LOUD,
JUST AS CLEAR,
JUST AS SWEET.

DUPLICATES INSTRUMENTAL MUSIC
WITH PERFECT
FIDELITY, TONE and
BRILLIANCY.

FILLS THE LARGEST AUDITORIUM OR CONCERT HALL AND NEVER FAILS TO CHARM ALL WHO HEAR IT

It is the talking machine long looked for, bringing the singer, the musician or the orchestra into the audible presence of the listener. Those familiar with other types, but who have never listened to the GRAPHOPHONE GRAND, have no conception of its wonders.

The numbers rendered, while strictly first class, will range from grave to gay and will consist of the LATEST MUSICAL SELECTIONS as played by GILMORE'S and SOUSA'S BANDS and the MOST FAMOUS ORCHESTRAS; VOCAL SELECTIONS by the MOST NOTED SINGERS—operatic, sentimental and comic. SPEECHES which in their startling reproduction will astound all present and can be heard as far or even farther than the original.

A CHOIR INVISIBLE. AN UNRIVALED MUSICAL FEAST.

Special arrangements have been made for magnifying the sound so that all may hear the entire concert while comfortably seated in any part of the hall. Don't fail to take advantage of this opportunity and be sure to bring the children, for it will please them more than anything that could be done for them.

PRICES OF ADMISSION: Adults_____ Children_____
EXHIBITION WILL BE GIVEN AT

Doors Open at_____

spreading jazz for two other reasons. First of all, the strident melodies and forceful rhythms of early jazz bands were better suited to mechanical recording than other types of music. Second, notation has no way of conveying the 'swing' which is so vital to jazz – it has to be learned by ear. If the bands could not be heard live, then there was no sheet music from which their music could be played at home on the piano. Records were an ideal way of getting round this difficulty.

The first jazz recording, made by the ODJB, was issued on 7 March 1917. The 'A' side was 'Dixieland Jazz Band One-Step' and the 'B' side 'Livery Stable Blues'. The 'B' side in particular became very popular, and the record sold over a million copies. For five years jazz and the record industry rose hand-in-hand. In 1921, for example, 100,000,000 records were produced. In 1922 the figure was 110,000,000. But 1922 was the year in which the 'radio boom' got under way, and radio hit the recording industry very hard.

Radio had two great advantages over records. The sound was smoother, and not as tinny or scratchy as that of mechanical recordings. Radio was also free once the receiving set had been bought. As a result radio became popular very quickly. The first radio station with scheduled programmes (KDKA Pittsburgh) went on the air in 1920. By 1922 there were over 200 radio stations and some 3,000,000 radio sets were in use. By 1926 the number of stations had risen to 694. Records sales went down sharply and in 1929 the Radio Corporation of America was able to buy out the Victor Talking Machine Company.

During the 1920s the majority of radio time was

An early radio

given over to the white commercial jazz described in this chapter. As a 1924 editorial in the magazine *Etude* put it: 'Listen in on the radio any night. Tap America anywhere in the air and nine times out of ten Jazz will burst forth.' Most of the jazz musicians who broadcast performed in front of radio station microphones. But after 1921 an increasing number broadcast direct from the dance floors of hotels and restaurants. This method of broadcasting was known as the 'remote hook-up'. Engineers simply laid a wire from the hotel or restaurant to the radio station. The 'hook-up' became especially popular since it allowed audiences to savour the atmosphere of sophisticated dance venues. After 1925, however, radio did not have to depend on the live broadcast. The advent of electronic recording made it possible for records to be put out live over the air waves.

During the first year or so, the 'radio' boom helped to spread jazz in much the same way as records. But there was one important difference between records and radio. While records were bought and played privately by individual people, radio was broadcast publicly over the air waves. With radio, therefore, the individual person had far less control over the music that could be heard in his own home. Because of this, there were moves to restrict the kinds of music that could be broadcast.

By today's standards, the censorship of music in the 1920s seems strong. The first song to be banned from radio, for instance, was 'Little Red Riding Hood', and this because of the line 'How could Little Red Riding Hood have been so very good and still keep the wolf from the door.' In another song, the line 'Silk stockings thrown aside' had to be changed to 'Gloves thrown aside'.

It would be wrong, however, to think that this attitude came about simply because of a concern with morals. There were also commercial reasons. From 1922 onwards most shows on American radio were 'sponsored'. A shop or a firm would pay for a show to be put on in return for 'exclusive' advertising time. This meant that only the sponsor could advertise on 'his' show. The last thing a sponsor wanted, of course, was to upset his audience. As a result 'hot' jazz and songs with 'offensive' words quickly disappeared.

But not all jazz was censored. 'Refined' jazz and dance band music survived. The general attitude at the time was summed up by one listener when he wrote that: 'the universal condemnation of jazz is contrary to the true feeling of a majority of radio listeners . . . would these objectors want to stop the broadcasting of such organisations as those of Paul Whiteman?'

6 Alleymen go West

Until about 1914 life in Tin Pan Alley was fairly straightforward. Songs were mass produced and plugged in vaudeville. White Americans bought the sheet music of songs made popular in vaudeville to play at home on the piano. Tin Pan Alley publishers made their money through the sale of sheet music, song-writers collected their royalties, and artists received gifts or a cut of the royalties in return for pushing songs in vaudeville. Tin Pan Alley was one big happy family.

By 1930 Tin Pan Alley had altered almost beyond recognition. The first real challenge to its way of life came from the dance venues. The Copyright Act of 1909 had given publishers and composers the right to collect royalties on songs that were performed publicly. However, it was impossible for publishers and composers to travel all over America collecting a few cents here and there every time a song was used in a dance arrangement. As a result, the publishers and composers very seldom received any money from live performances of their music. So, in 1914, the publishers and composers of Tin Pan Alley formed the American Society of Composers, Authors and Publishers (ASCAP). This society immediately took Shanley's Restaurant in New York to court for not paying royalties on the music of one of its members. A long court case followed, and, in 1917, Supreme Court Judge Wendell Holmes ruled in favour of ASCAP. Royalties on live performances in restaurants, hotels and ballrooms had to be paid. From 1921 onwards the members of ASCAP were able to collect those royalties.

As they became more popular, records drew audiences away from vaudeville and caused a slump in the sales of sheet music. Vaudeville managers put up signs in theatres warning artists that 'Recording harms your throat'. Yet, as a rule, Tin Pan Alley and the recording industry got on quite well together. Tin Pan Alley publishers collected a two per cent royalty on any song of theirs that was recorded, and vaudeville managers were still able to draw audiences by putting recording stars into their acts.

However, the real villain of the piece in the eyes of Tin Pan Alley was the radio. Records and dance venues had cut into vaudeville's audiences as well as causing a reduction in the sales of sheet music. But with radio, the death of vaudeville was unavoidable. It was much easier to stay at home and listen to the stars than to go to a vaudeville theatre and hear a possibly second-rate performance. Radio thus replaced vaudeville as the central market-place for songs. It also replaced sheet music and the piano as the main source of home entertainment. Its great sin, however, was to refuse to pay any royalties on the music it used. Once again ASCAP went to the courts and won. The society received a percentage of radio's profits and, in exchange, gave radio the right to perform any of its member's music over the air waves.

An important effect of radio was to create a gap between performers and the public. In the days of vaudeville there were a great number of performers, and they had close contact with their audiences across the footlights of vaudeville theatres. Performers knew at once whether they were a success or failure with a particular audience, for example. But with radio the great variety of entertainment offered by the different vaudeville theatres was absent. The same radio programme went into every home, to be heard by hundreds of thousands of people rather than just a few hundred (as was the case with the individual vaudeville performance). As a result, a small number of 'stars' such as Kate Smith, Russ Colombo and Rudy Vallee were born. They were known by a great number of people, but had very little direct contact with any of them.

Songs that were written with radio and the big stars in mind became different from those produced in vaudeville days. In those days a song just had to appeal to enough people to make the publishing of sheet music worth while (although, of course, many songs returned very handsome profits indeed). Also, a song could be expected to stay popular and sell for well over a year, thus bringing in money over a long period of time. With radio, however, a song had to appeal to *everyone* (since the same music went into every home). It also had to appeal to them *immediately*. Because radio did go into such a great number of homes it could make a hit in seven days and kill it in sixty, much as it does today. A song thus had to be easy to listen to as well as being something most people would like to hear. As a result, songs changed in character from the earlier vaudeville days.

You will remember that in 'A Bird in a Gilded Cage', we saw how the sadness of a woman who

married for money and could no longer have love
was told through a story. The moral of the story was
also plainly spelt out:

> 'Tis sad when you think of her wasted life,
> For youth cannot mate with age,
> And her beauty was sold for an old man's gold,
> She's a bird in a gilded cage.

In contrast to this, songs of the late 1920s and early
1930s tend to paint pictures rather than tell stories,
however. The 1927 song 'My Blue Heaven' is about
a husband, his wife and baby, all of whom have a
happy home life. Yet the first verse is about birds
who go back to the shelter of their nest at night:

> Day is ending
> Birds are wending
> Back to the shelter of
> Each little love nest they love.

Such a verse is known as a 'parallel' for the main
idea – a husband going home to his wife and child at
night. The actions of the bird parallel, that is, are the
same type of thing as, the actions of the husband.
This becomes more obvious in the chorus. But the
lyricist did not call the husband's home 'my home'.
He called it 'my blue heaven'.

> When Whipourwills call and evening is nigh
> I hurry to my blue heaven.
> A turn to the right, a little white light
> Will lead you to my blue heaven.
> You'll see a smiling face, a fireplace, a cosy room,
> A little nest that's nestled where the roses bloom.
> Just Mollie and me
> And baby makes three,
> We're happy in my blue heaven.

Most important, however, is the mood of the lyric. The picture of the house is not brilliant and fashionable, like the setting of 'Gilded Cage'. Instead, it is very cosy; there is a 'little white light', a 'fireplace', a 'cosy room' and, above all, 'Mollie and me/And baby makes three.' The setting is also very romantic. The song opens with a description of birds and continues with the soft call of the whipourwill bird. It is evening – a traditional time for romance – and the house is set among roses; it could be an old thatched cottage. It is a beautiful but idealised picture since, as we know, by this time the large majority of Americans lived in bustling, modern cities. But it is a way of putting across home life which can still be seen any evening in adverts on commercial television.

Changes in lyrics were also reflected in the music, which required flowing tunes and soft, restless harmonies. The old style gave way to a new one, which needed more skill and was beyond most of the old-style Alley writers. Composers had to play with more than one finger, deal with difficult harmonies, know about arranging, as well as be able to write down some of the jazz elements which had crept into Tin Pan Alley songs. As a result, very few writers survived into the days of radio and, subsequently, film. The one notable exception was Irving Berlin.

Broadway

The old-style Alley writers were gradually replaced by more and more Broadway composers. Broadway was, and still is, the home of American musical theatre. But what is musical theatre?

Musical theatre grew out of American vaudeville and European operetta, which is a kind of light-hearted opera. Vaudeville theatres put on the

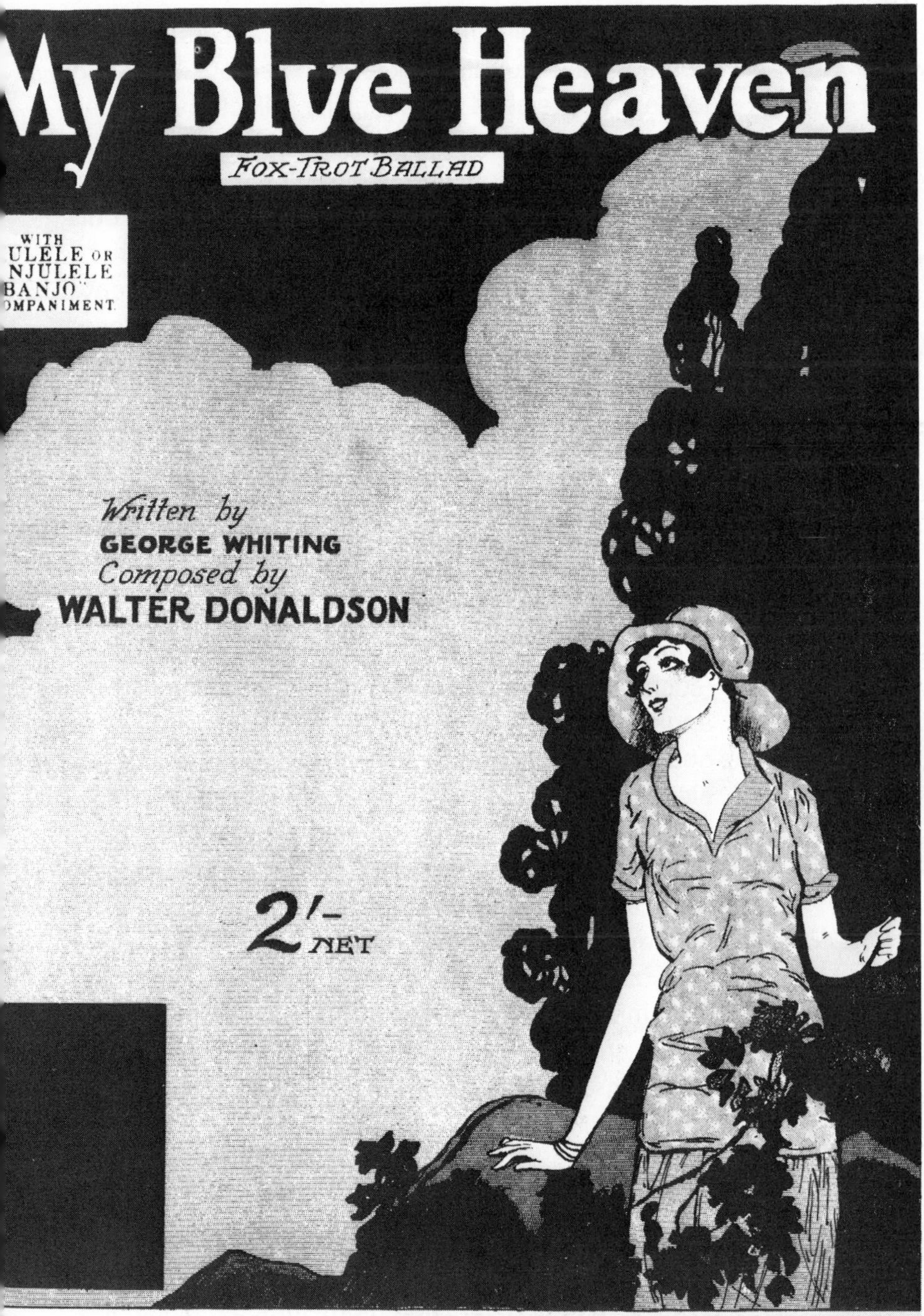

nt

PRINTED IN ENGLAND.

different speciality acts of singers, dancers, comedians, acrobats, jugglers and so on. The songs, jokes and sketches of vaudeville reflected everyday life in ordinary language, but were not connected by any underlying story-line. Operetta was very different. It had a story which ran from beginning to end, but the story would be highly fanciful, written in high-flown language, and have little to do with everyday life. Operettas tended to be about imaginary princes and princesses living in far away imaginary countries like Ruritania. Typical of these was *The Student Prince*. Unlike vaudeville, operettas also had a great deal of elaborate classical music.

Along with vaudeville, the higher-class European operetta was very popular in late-nineteenth-century America. But by the turn of the century American composers quite understandably wanted to write their own American 'operetta'. At first these composers (such as Victor Herbert and the team of Rudolf Friml and Sigmund Romberg) did little but copy European operetta. Words and music were elaborate, and the stories had little to do with the world of the average white American. Gradually, however, the imitation European operetta turned into the American stage musical by drawing on the tradition of American vaudeville.

Showboat, which opened on Broadway on 27 December 1927, provided the first striking example of this change. The story of *Showboat* is set in the southern United States, and touches on the harsh life of the black people who lived there. The words and lyrics (written by Oscar Hammerstein II) are in a language which every white American would have understood, and the music (by Jerome Kern) is typical of American popular music of the time. *Showboat* in fact contains many famous songs, the most memorable of which is 'Ol' Man River'.

But although *Showboat* told an American story
through American words and music, it still presented
its songs a bit like speciality acts. There would be a
dramatic scene followed by a song, which would be
followed by another dramatic scene followed by a
song, and so on. Songs could also be taken out of
the show without really disturbing the story. *Porgy
and Bess*, which opened on Broadway on 10
October 1935, changed this. The show (written by
George Gershwin, Ira Gershwin and DuBose
Heyward) was nearly all song, and, with the
exception of the very famous 'Summertime', all the
songs added something to the drama. Story and
music were much more closely tied to one another.

Finally, in March 1943, came *Oklahoma!* Written
by Oscar Hammerstein II and Richard Rodgers,
Oklahoma! was the first stage musical where words,
lyrics, song and dance *all* played second fiddle to the
overall action. *Nothing* was put in the show unless it
added something to the story or drama. Also, there
were to be no left-overs from the days of vaudeville.
Dances and songs had to take place naturally as
part of the musical's story, and not as if they still had
something of the speciality act left in them.
Oklahoma's director, Rouben Mamoulian, would not
let characters come to the front of the stage to
'present' their songs, for example. The songs had to
be sung as the characters moved round the stage as
part of the action.

Mamoulian, who had been greatly influenced by
Porgy and Bess, described his attitude towards a
musical's song and dance in the following way:

Normally . . . you had a dramatic scene, people
talking. Then, suddenly, one of them got up and

Oklahoma!, the 'integrated' musical. Dancing and singing go on at the same time, and singers do not 'present' to the audience

started singing. A convention, but it was ridiculous. Or another scene, comedy perhaps, when suddenly, *boom*! a dancer is pounding round the stage. It's idiotic. But suppose you had a dramatic scene with a rising emotion where *nothing* could top the spoken words except a song? Or, in dramatic action, you bring it to as big a climax as you can, which inevitably leads to a dance . . . This integration of form is essential.

Oklahoma! was the first 'integrated' musical play, and it set the seal on the American stage musical. The songs, dances, jokes and stories of American vaudeville had been mixed with the overall form of European operetta to give America a new kind of entertainment. But this new entertainment required a different kind of composer from those who wrote the old-style Alley hit tunes. There was a tremendous difference, for example, between writing 'Tea for Two' and putting together the entire musical score for productions such as *Porgy and Bess* or *Oklahoma!* It is not surprising that nearly all the famous Broadway composers (Jerome Kern, Richard Rodgers, George Gershwin, Cole Porter) had some training in classical music. Some, such as Kern, Rodgers and Porter, also went to university. Irving Berlin was the only real exception. During his entire life he was only able to play in one key, that of F sharp major.

Perhaps the most remarkable of the composers who put the American musical firmly on the map was George Gershwin (1898–1937). Like Irving Berlin, Gershwin had started out in Tin Pan Alley and vaudeville. At the age of fifteen he became a plugger for the Jerome H. Remick Music Publishing Company. He then moved on to become a vaudeville accompanist and, after that, a rehearsal pianist for the musical *Miss 1917*. (A rehearsal pianist provides the music for a show while it is being rehearsed. The orchestra is not usually brought in until a day or two before the dress rehearsal.)

During his time as a rehearsal pianist Gershwin was noticed by another publisher, Max Dreyfus, who hired him as a regular staff composer. A year later, in 1918, Gershwin wrote one of his most famous songs, 'Swanee' (the lyricist was Irving Caesar). Although not intended for inclusion in a musical, the song so impressed Al Jolson that he had it put in *Sinbad*, a show in which he was then starring. This ensured the song's success.

But although Gershwin started out in Tin Pan Alley, he was not, like Irving Berlin, one of its major figures. Gershwin had also received considerable training as a classical pianist as well as some instruction in music theory before entering the Alley. These talents were soon to emerge in a series of musical comedies (many of the lyrics being written by his elder brother Ira Gershwin) and in several notable concert pieces – all jazz influenced. The first of these pieces was *Rhapsody in Blue*, composed in 1924 for Paul Whiteman (see chapter 5). *Rhapsody in Blue* was followed in 1925 by the piano *Concerto in F*, and, in 1928, by the orchestral piece *An American in Paris*.

Gershwin's career climaxed in 1935 with the production of his *Porgy and Bess*. Not only were words and music more closely tied together in *Porgy and Bess* than in any previous musical. The show also came closer to being a full-scale opera than any American stage musical before or since. In many ways *Porgy and Bess* could be thought of as the sort of success Scott Joplin was aiming at twenty-four years earlier.

Throughout his career George Gershwin demonstrated a remarkable breadth of talent. At one extreme he was the writer of popular songs. At the other he was the composer of an operatic musical and several 'classical' concert pieces. It was a great loss to the musical world when he died unexpectedly of a brain tumour in 1937.

Hollywood

Radio (and, to a lesser extent, records) had destroyed the old Tin Pan Alley by coming between it and its audience. Together, they had given rise to the big isolated star, and so created a totally different market for the writers of popular songs. These songs now came more and more from Broadway musicals or were written by composers with some Broadway

experience. They still had their roots in the sentimental ballads and the different kinds of Afro-American music that Tin Pan Alley had taken over, but were now given a touch of sophistication drawn from the world of classical music.

Tin Pan Alley had survived these changes from a financial point of view, but the battle had been tough. Many publishing houses had been badly affected. Towards the end of the 1920s a great number were taken over by the big Hollywood movie companies.

Why should West Coast movie companies be interested in East Coast publishing houses? Today, we have got used to the idea that most films are dramas with background music to give the right atmosphere. Film musicals such as *Oliver!* are now the exception rather than the rule. But films were not always like this. Before 1927 they were all silent, and featured such stars as Charlie Chaplin, Buster Keaton and that great romantic actor, Rudolph Valentino. Because the films were silent, live music had to be provided in the cinema to accompany the action on the screen. The music was usually played on the piano or the mighty Wurlitzer organ, and less often by rag bands or orchestras.

Right from the beginning, therefore, film and music were inseparable. So much was this so that when 'talking pictures' became possible in the mid-1920s, many film companies thought audiences would not like them. As a result, the first 'talking picture' was not really a talking picture at all, but a film musical. *The Jazz Singer*, starring Al Jolson, was released in 1927 by Warner Brothers. It was an immediate success. Two years later, in 1929, thirty-two film musicals were released, and the future of the 'talking picture' was safe.

opposite
The human
waterfall of
Footlight Parade

Film musicals need songs, of course, and it was mainly for this reason that Hollywood began to take over Tin Pan Alley. It was not long, for example, before Warner Brothers owned the copyrights on most of Jerome Kern's, Richard Rodgers's, George Gershwin's and Cole Porter's songs. All these composers moved out to the West Coast, as did some old-style Alley song-writers. But, for the Broadway composers, it was not a happy experience.

Broadway composers found Hollywood frustrating because it was not in business to produce 'integrated' musicals. Like radio, the Hollywood musical went out to a mass audience. Also like radio, it therefore had to appeal to everyone and to appeal to them immediately. Most film musicals consequently became little more than excuses for presenting the public with songs. Plots were weak and the characters seemed more like cardboard cut-outs than real people. But the songs were very sophisticated. They were skilfully composed and much more subtle in both music and lyrics. In general, the lyrics were of what became known as the 'moonlight and roses' type – romantic, rich and beautiful in subject and setting.

Hollywood's job was simply to put this new type of Tin Pan Alley song on film. A few films did this very well, however, especially those in which the dance director Busby Berkeley had a hand. Berkeley used to illustrate the themes of songs with very carefully planned dance sequences featuring large choruses of girls. He was also noted for his clever use of the camera. In *Footlight Parade* (released in 1933), for example, Berkeley illustrated the song 'By a Waterfall' with a chorus of 100 girls. The sequence was filmed mainly from overhead, with the girls

opposite
The beautifully poised Fred Astaire and his long-standing partner Ginger Rogers

making human patterns in a pool and on an hydraulic fountain.

Busby Berkeley's genius can only be properly understood by watching one of his films (they are still shown on television today). The same can be said of the film musicals which starred the most famous dancing team of all time, Fred Astaire and Ginger Rogers. This couple made nine films together during the 1930s. After making *The Story of Vernon and Irene Castle* in 1939 they split up (although they did reunite for one more film in 1949), and Fred Astaire went on to dance with such famous film stars as Rita Hayworth and Audrey Hepburn.

Fred Astaire's dancing is notable for its elegance and smoothness. The same is true of his singing, and it surprises many people that Broadway composers thought of Astaire as one of the best interpreters of their songs. Indeed, it was while working on Astaire–Rogers films that Jerome Kern, Irving Berlin and George Gershwin had some of their most rewarding moments in Hollywood.

By the early 1930s, film musicals had become established. They had also completely finished vaudeville. White Americans now either went to the movies for their entertainment or stayed at home and listened to the radio. A great number of hit songs came from film musicals and were plugged on the radio as part of an effort to get movie audiences.

It was thus possible for the film industry and radio to work hand-in-hand to a certain extent. However, the fact that radio had to pay large sums of money to ASCAP (and so, now, to Hollywood) for the music it used continued to cause resentment. The situation reached a crisis in 1941. This crisis is described in chapter 8.

7 It don't mean a thing

Depression In October 1929, the economy of the United States
collapsed. The Depression, as it was known, lasted
into the 1930s. It threw millions of people out of
work and created widespread hardship on a scale
that is hard to imagine today.

As we saw in chapter 5, 'hot' white jazz was in a
firm decline by the end of the 1920s. However, the
Depression spelt trouble for the *whole* of the white
jazz movement that had so successfully reflected the
gay and sophisticated spirit of the times. There was
now very little to be gay or lively about. People
wanted entertainment that soothed them and took
their minds off their troubles. One way of getting this
relief was to listen to the 'moonlight and roses' songs
broadcast over the radio. It is said that people would
go hungry rather than part with their precious radio
sets. Another was to go to the cinema and see the
film fantasies put out by Hollywood. Busby Berkeley,
for instance, saw it as his job to relieve people of
their everyday cares. 'In the era of breadlines,
Depression and wars,' he said, 'I tried to help people
get away from all the misery . . . to turn their minds
to something else. I wanted to make people happy,
if only for an hour.'

While other industries were collapsing, therefore,
the entertainment industry was doing very well for

itself. But the Depression did not last for ever. In 1933, Franklin D. Roosevelt became President of the United States and put into effect the 'New Deal'. This was a huge government programme that gave people jobs and helped to get the economy on its feet again. People gradually became more confident and once more felt able to look towards the future. The escapism of Tin Pan Alley songs and Hollywood film spectaculars was no longer quite so important. Younger people in particular wanted something that was more in tune with the times.

The new development came yet again from black American music – in this case, jazz. White musicians had for some years admired black jazz musicians and had gone to hear them when they could. As the famous Swing bandleader Artie Shaw put it:

> Whenever I got a week off I'd go up to Chicago and sit at the feet – literally at the feet – of these guys, on the edge of the bandstand, and watch these cats like Louis Armstrong doing what he was doing.

Goodman and Swing

On the evening of 21 August 1935, in the Palomar Ballroom, Los Angeles, white clarinettist Benny Goodman led his band in playing some of the hottest music they had. Many of the numbers, such as 'King Porter Stomp', had been arranged by black bandleader Fletcher Henderson. The audience went wild, and radio hook-ups did the rest. 'Swing' had arrived.

What exactly was 'Swing'? Like ragtime and jazz it was partly a type of music, and partly a label for a period in the history of American popular entertainment. Swing grew out of the attempts of black bandleaders such as Fletcher Henderson to marry the improvisation and swing of New Orleans jazz to the sound of the big band.

Big bands had three sections: the brass section (trumpets and trombones), the reed section (saxophones and clarinets), and the rhythm section (drums, piano, guitar, and a string bass or tuba). With this greater number of musicians (Fletcher Henderson's band had ten musicians as opposed to the more normal seven or eight of a New Orleans band) *completely free* improvisation was very difficult, if not impossible. As a result, musical numbers for big bands had to be arranged and notated. But this arranging and notation did not, as was the case with Paul Whiteman's band, prevent *all* improvisation. Rather, the different sections and soloists in a band all had an allotted time in an arrangement when they could show off their different playing skills.

However, having arrangements for a large number of musicians, grouped in sections, made new problems. The rhythmic 'swing' and excitement of jazz had previously been created by individual musicians. Could so subtle an effect be kept when several musicians played together as a section? Henderson found the answer to this problem – how to make notated jazz swing – and consequently made his band a great success with black audiences.

The swing and improvisation of Henderson's music was largely preserved by Benny Goodman, and that is what made his band so different from that of Paul Whiteman's. However, Goodman's band preserved less of the blues elements of the 1920s' black jazz bands. Goodman had had some training in classical music, and it was possibly this that led him to cut out most of the blues techniques that had their origin in rural blues singing. In this way Goodman could be said to form the same sort of link between 1920s' black jazz and 1930s' white commercial Swing as the ODJB did between black New Orleans jazz and white dance bands such as Paul Whiteman's. Like the ODJB, Goodman made black jazz understandable for white audiences.

The swing and improvisation of Goodman's band was enough to make the 1920s' dance bands sound old-fashioned, and this is exactly what young people in the mid-1930s wanted. As the 1932 popular song put it: 'It Don't Mean a Thing If It Ain't Got That Swing'. Young people all over America flocked to hear the Swing bands that sprang up after Goodman's 1935 success. They crammed into theatres and cinemas, and jitterbugged and jived to the music of Artie Shaw, the Dorsey Brothers and Harry James. They also invented their own private language or 'jive-talk'. Girls became 'chicks', and people who liked Swing were 'cats'. Anything that was good was 'hep'. Finally, the young followers of Swing began to worship the 'sidemen' or famous jazzmen featured in improvised solos with the different bands. These sidemen, such as Gene Krupa (Benny Goodman's drummer) and Bud Freeman (Tommy Dorsey's tenor saxophone player), became stars in their own right and were often traded between bands in much the same way as modern football players. Some, such as Gene Krupa, went on to start their own bands.

Tin Pan Alley could not afford to miss this fervour and excitement. Swing bands were recorded and did countless radio shows. And with the dancing, the 'jive-talk' and the worship of sidemen, Swing ceased to be a particular kind of jazz, and became another Tin Pan Alley fashion. Any type of music could be made into Swing. ' "Swing" ', in the words of Artie Shaw, 'became just another of the labels given to the mass market of popular music.'

There was a great deal of money to be made during the Swing era, but many bandleaders found the going tough. There were endless one-night stands, with the same numbers being played in exactly the same way to please the audience. It was as if the music was being pre-packaged and taken round the country to be sold like food on a supermarket shelf. Everybody knew what was coming and what to expect.

Late in 1939, the pressure became too much for Artie Shaw, who was possibly the Swing era's most musically brilliant white bandleader (his most successful number was 'Begin the Beguine' – a 1935 Cole Porter number). He left the bandstand in the middle of a concert, and went off to Mexico for a rest. The reasons he gave for his unusual action show what must have been in the minds of many Swing bandleaders. The majority of these bandleaders were fine jazz musicians, and knew perfectly well what they were doing in tailoring their music for the needs of Tin Pan Alley. As Shaw said:

> I couldn't stand debasing my music so that it could be understood by a mass audience who didn't know what I was doing. And finally, you've got to come down to people's level for them to understand and stay with you. Your agent and your manager and your publicity man and your fan club will tell you that you've got to compromise. So the music gets to be pap, and when it gets to be pap, you've had it. Music is one thing and business is another.

In order to get some relief from commercial Swing,

some bandleaders formed very small groups out of their bands to play the sort of jazz *they* liked. These were often known as 'the band within the band'. It is interesting, for example, that Artie Shaw formed his Gramercy Five after his return from Mexico in 1940. However, the best-known of these small groups was the Goodman Quartet. This had a special place in the history of Afro-American music, since it was the first group in which black *and* white musicians appeared together on the same stage. The white members were Goodman (clarinet) and Gene Krupa (drums), and the black were Teddy Wilson (piano) and Lionel Hampton (vibraharp). Graham Vulliamy describes the type of opposition which black musicians faced in *Jazz and Blues*. However, when promoters saw how enthusiastic audiences were they were willing to go along with Goodman. Though this by no means solved the problem of racial discrimination in American music, before long many Swing bands (including those of Artie Shaw and Woody Herman) had black musicians among their numbers. An important step had been taken towards breaking down racial barriers.

Glenn Miller   Without doubt, the most successful commercial white bandleader was Glenn Miller. Miller was born on 1 March 1904, in Clarinda, Iowa, a small town in the mid-west of America. In 1925, he joined the Ben Pollack Band as a trombonist. Though only an average trombonist, he had there the opportunity to develop his skills as an arranger. He left this band in 1928 and, until he started forming his first band in 1936, Miller continued to work as a trombonist and arranger with practically every bandleader of note. It was during this time that his arrangements began to take on a personal style in which everything was carefully planned out and rehearsed. This craftsmanship is what makes his most well-known arrangements (like 'In the Mood' and 'String of Pearls') still popular today.

By 1936 Miller had a very good sense of what he wanted from a band. He was also tired of working for other people, so the natural step was to form a band of his own. The Glenn Miller Orchestra first played publicly in the spring of 1937. In the beginning it was very successful. However, this success was short-lived, and in January 1938 the band split up.

Why had this happened? Probably because the band had no style or personality. All the other great Swing bandleaders of the time (Goodman, Shaw, Tommy Dorsey, James, Krupa and Teagarden, for example) were famous players in their own right. Their bands were built round them, and they were big stars with whom the public could identify. Miller, unfortunately, did not come across as a big personality, and the only way the band could have succeeded was by having a very distinctive sound. That sound was not yet there. However, it *was* to come with the formation of his second band, in March 1938.

Glenn Miller came across the distinctive sound of his arrangements by accident. Before forming his first band, he had worked for an English bandleader, Ray Noble, who was working in America. Noble had a trumpet player, Peewee Erwin, who was very keen on playing high notes. As a result, Miller wrote parts for Erwin which few other trumpeters could play, since they were much higher in pitch than usual. Unfortunately, Erwin left the band. Rather than rewrite all his arrangements, Miller simply replaced the high trumpet with a clarinet. Clarinets can play from the same music as trumpets, as well as play high notes very easily.

In a Swing band, it had been usual for the brass section to play higher notes than the reed section. Because the clarinet had replaced the lead trumpet, Miller realised that this need not be so, and it was this difference that was the basis of his famous sound. The four saxophones of his second band played above the brass section, and were themselves topped off by a single clarinet. The result was sweet, smooth, cosy and somewhat treacly. Probably the most famous example of this sound, which you can often hear on the radio, is to be found in the opening of the Miller band's signature tune, 'Moonlight Serenade'.

Miller had his sound. His second band also started playing at a time when commercial Swing was very much on the rise. Yet success was not quick. It is always difficult to be successful with a second band, especially when the first has been a failure. Slowly, however, public recognition came. In May 1939, the band started an engagement at the Glen Island Casino which lasted for fourteen weeks. Audiences were wildly enthusiastic. Once again, live radio broadcasts did the rest.

The Glenn Miller Orchestra dominated Swing from 1939 until 1942, when Miller went into the American Army. America had entered the Second World War against Germany and Japan in 1941, and the bandleader, having had a strict upbringing, felt he ought to do his bit. Rather than wait to be drafted (or forced) into the Army like so many other Swing musicians, he volunteered. Very soon he had formed an Army band that was as famous as the Glenn Miller Orchestra. It performed at home and then, in 1944, went to England to entertain the troops. In

November 1944 Miller was ordered to take his band to France. He set off to fly the English Channel on 15 December, a particularly foggy day. The small plane in which just he and another man were flying was never heard of again.

The Swing era was remarkable for the youth of its fans. It was the first time in the history of Tin Pan Alley that a fashion had come about almost solely because of teenage support. It was also the first time that one musician had been treated rather like a god. The adulation Miller received was only later to be equalled by that heaped on figures such as Frank Sinatra, Elvis Presley and the Beatles. When Miller died, however, the Swing era itself did not have long to live. To understand why, it is necessary to continue the story of the ASCAP–radio dispute already mentioned in chapter 6.

8 Bobbysox and Blue eyes

**Confron-
tation and
strike**

Chapter 6 described how ASCAP took the radio
companies to court in order to get royalties for the
music of its members that was played over the air
waves. Although radio companies did not like paying
the money, they got on quite well with Tin Pan Alley
and ASCAP once the court cases had been decided.
When Hollywood took over many of the ASCAP
publishing houses this uneasy co-operation
continued. Hollywood had hit songs plugged on radio
to get audiences for film musicals. Radio played the
songs because people were keen to hear the big
stars (such as Fred Astaire and Dick Powell) who
sang in these Hollywood spectaculars.

This co-operation suited both sides as long as they
were both making money. However, towards the end
of the 1930s Swing began to affect Hollywood. All
radio had to do to profit from Swing was to arrange
hook-ups from theatres and dance venues,
broadcast the records of the big Swing bands, and
put on 'live' radio shows. These were things that
radio had been doing for over ten years.

Hollywood, unfortunately, was not nearly so well
prepared for Swing. The only way it could cash in on
the new entertainment fashion was to make films
about the famous Swing bands. Films take much
longer, are much more costly, and much more

difficult to make than radio shows. These difficulties also become worse when the principal characters of a film are musicians (such as Benny Goodman and Harry James) with little knowledge of acting. Although Hollywood did bring Swing music to the ears of white Americans, therefore, it could not do it as quickly or as well as radio.

As a result, the number of people going to Hollywood movies went down and with it Hollywood's profit. The only thing Hollywood could do was to attack the rival who was taking the audiences. Through ASCAP, Hollywood planned to raise the royalties paid by radio to such an extent that one of two things would happen. If radio could not afford the royalties, it would have little popular music to play, and audiences would go back to the cinema. If, on the other hand, radio could afford the royalties, Hollywood would not suffer financially through the loss of audiences.

ASCAP and Hollywood had, however, made one basic mistake. ASCAP thought that the only popular music white Americans would want to listen to was the music owned by itself. But this proved not to be so. Towards the end of the 1930s, radio got wind of ASCAP's plans and started to build up a collection of music not covered by ASCAP copyright. In 1939, the radio companies set up their own copyright company, Broadcast Music Incorporated (BMI). By the time ASCAP announced their new royalty rates for 1941, BMI owned a lot of music.

The royalties ASCAP wanted from radio in January 1941 were double what they had previously been. Radio refused to pay, and as a result no ASCAP music could be played over the air waves. But instead of sending audiences back to the cinema, the ban on ASCAP music simply meant that people now heard BMI-owned music. As we shall see in chapter 10, this created a great deal of interest in what we now know as 'country and western', and 'rhythm and blues' music. Americans liked the change, and, in October 1941, ASCAP was forced to climb down and settle with the radio companies.

While ASCAP and BMI were arguing with each other in 1941, another dispute was brewing up. This time it was between the American Federation of Musicians (AFoM) and the record companies. The musicians wanted more money for making records. Unlike radio and the cinema, the record industry had suffered during the Depression. Records were more expensive than radio (which was free once the radio set had been bought), and were not as good as films at taking people's minds off their troubles. However, when the Depression lifted the record industry picked up. The public bought more records. Records were also being used in greater and greater numbers by radio and by the jukeboxes which had sprung up all over America during the 1930s.

The musicians who made records deserved much more money. Not only were more records being sold. They were also being played much more. However, the record companies did not want to pay the money, and so, on 1 August 1942, AFoM went on strike. No musicians belonging to AFoM were allowed to record. This strike went on until October 1943 when, starved of new records, the record companies gave in and settled with the union.

The death of Swing and the rise of the vocalist

Both disputes had important consequences for the history of white popular music in America. One of these consequences was the decline of Tin Pan Alley itself. This is described in chapter 10. Two others will be discussed now, however. They are the decline of Swing and the rise of the solo vocalist.

The end of the Swing era can be dated as January 1947, when no less than eight top Swing bands broke up. Among them were those of Benny Goodman, Harry James, Tommy Dorsey and Jack Teagarden. This collapse of Swing took place for many reasons. In *Jazz and Blues*, Graham Vulliamy refers to the harmful effects that the Second World War had on many Swing bands, as well as to the rise of be-bop, a new and exciting style of jazz. However, it is the ASCAP–BMI dispute and the AFoM strike which are the more important from our point of view. Because most of their music was ASCAP-owned, the Swing bands were not much heard on the radio during 1941. Moreover, they were not able to record during the fifteen months of the AFoM strike. Deprived of their familiar Swing bands many white Americans began to enjoy other kinds of popular music. This, of course, ate into the popularity of the Swing bands. Yet matters were made much worse by the fact that the vocalists of Swing bands, who were not members of AFoM, were able to continue recording during the AFoM strike.

Singers had played a central part in the life of Tin Pan Alley ever since the early days of vaudeville. Yet, perhaps surprisingly, it was quite some time before they became a regular feature of dance bands. It in fact took the clever business sense of Paul Whiteman to realise what an advantage singers could be. Singers lent a more personal touch to these big musical organisations than individual leaders, and they therefore helped people identify more easily with the particular style of different bands. When Whiteman hired The Rhythm Boys in 1926 (Bing Crosby was one of the three singers who made up this group), he started a trend that was to be copied by nearly all the Swing bands. But because the job of the singers was to put over the personality of the band as a whole rather than their own personality as individual star vocalists, they were not thought to be as important as other musicians. For this reason the 'crooners' and 'canaries' (as men and women vocalists came to be known) were often paid less than sidemen and section men. However, crooners and canaries became more and more popular during the late 1930s, and, by the early 1940s, some of them had become the main attraction of the star bands.

One of them in particular had become very famous. Frank Sinatra had started work with the Harry James band in 1939. In 1940 he moved to Tommy Dorsey's Orchestra, where he quickly gained a vast following among white Americans. By 1942, he had become more popular than his own bandleader. This state of affairs could not possibly last, and so, on 10 September 1942, Sinatra left the Dorsey band to go it alone. By this time the AFoM strike had begun, and all the band singers were free to record on their own. When the strike ended, many vocalists had made it as solo stars, and no longer needed Swing bands to promote them. The emergence of the solo vocalist was thus one more nail in the coffin of Swing.

For most people, Frank Sinatra is one of the greatest popular singers of all time. He can also claim to be one of the world's greatest entertainers. As we shall see, Sinatra had an impressive career as a movie actor as well as being a great singer. It is, however, impossible to appreciate Sinatra's greatness as a singer without knowing something about the development of popular singing during this century. This development can best be described by talking a little about two other great popular singers, Al Jolson and Bing Crosby.

Jolie   The art of popular singing in America goes back at least to the time of Henry Russell, the English baritone mentioned in chapter 2. As we saw in chapter 2, most white popular singers of the nineteenth century travelled with different kinds of troupes, the most important of which were the blackface minstrel shows. It was from such a background that Al Jolson came. He moved from circuses and minstrel shows to vaudeville, where he began to make a name for himself around 1909. By 1911 he was an established vaudeville entertainer.

The secret of Jolson's success as an entertainer was that, like Russell, he had a tremendous emotional affect upon audiences. He was only really happy when he was on the stage. As a result, Jolson did not give straightforward performances. He was always trying to woo an audience, to keep it in the palm of his hand. This is what lay behind his famous catchphrase, 'Wait a minute, wait a minute! You ain't heard nothin' yet.' The desire to keep an audience in a theatre as long as possible also explains his singing style. When Jolson sang, he did not simply deliver the notes and words as they were written down. He half-sang and half-spoke songs as if their message were meant for every single person in the audience.

The larger-than-life Al Jolson in full costume

It was this half-singing, half-speaking way of getting songs across that made Jolson important for every American popular singer who followed him. He loved words, pulling them about to extract every ounce of meaning, as he does, for example, in 'Sonny Boy'. In this, his singing had something in common with the rural blues mentioned in chapter 4. It is thus not surprising that the songs Jolson had most success with were 'coon' songs, a kind of Tin Pan Alley ballad that had grown out of the ragtime heard in minstrel shows. The song which best demonstrates Jolson's background in minstrel shows is 'My Mammy'. This 'coon' song, which gave rise to a big spate of blackface 'mammy' songs, first became popular in 1918.

Jolson, who usually performed in blackface wearing a pair of white gloves, continued to work until his death in 1950. However, the period that really belongs to him is that of 1911 to the mid-1920s. Once the microphone came along with the arrival of radio and electronic recording, Jolson found it difficult to compete with other singers. There was a great difference between making oneself heard at the back of a theatre without a microphone, and singing into a microphone so that one's voice did not 'boom' or distort. The first kind of singing requires a loud and clear voice, the second a quieter and more intimate 'crooning' style. Jolson was unable to make this change. As he said in 1932: 'This radio business is not for Jolie.' 'It's a sad day,' he went on, 'when Jolie needs a mike to sing into.'

The Groaner

Al Jolson's importance lay in bringing an Afro-American approach to white popular singing of this century. In their different ways, every white American popular singer after him was to learn to bend and stretch notes to get as much meaning as possible out of the lyrics. The importance of Bing Crosby (nicknamed 'The Groaner') lay in marrying this Afro-American approach with singing through a microphone. Jolson was Crosby's first singing model. Yet Crosby's style was exactly the opposite of Jolson's. While Jolson's performances were boisterous and his singing exaggerated, Bing Crosby ended up presenting himself as an ordinary man, or 'ordinary Joe'. This is apparent in his singing of 'White Christmas', the 1942 hit mentioned earlier in this book in connection with Irving Berlin. He has talked about this image himself. 'I think,' said Crosby, 'that every man who . . . listens to my records, or who hears me on the radio, believes firmly that he sings as well as I do, especially when he's in the bathroom . . . It's no trick for him to believe this,' Crosby continued, 'because I have none of the mannerisms of a trained singer, and I have very little voice.'

Crosby, in fact, was being very modest. It is true that, compared to some other singers, he had very little voice. But what he had he learnt to use to the full. Before the microphone came along, he managed to project his voice with great effect, as fellow singer Rudy Vallee relates. In 1927, Vallee went to Baltimore to hear Paul Whitemen and the Rhythm Boys. 'Suddenly,' Vallee recounts, 'one of [the Rhythm Boys] walked to the center of the floor and delivered a popular song of the day . . . There was no amplifying system in those days, and I could scarcely hear his rendition. When he had finished, there was a deafening roar of applause.'

Bing Crosby succeeded with his small voice in pre-microphone days because he had learnt from Al Jolson and others exactly how to get the best out of

opposite
Crosby with his comedian partner Bob Hope, in *The Road to Singapore*

lyrics and tunes. When the microphone came along this success continued. Crosby sang into it as if he were singing *to just one person*. As a radio announcer of the time said, Bing 'sounds as if he were leaning over the piano in your parlor singing to you.' It was because of his 'ordinary' and intimate style that Bing Crosby quickly became the best loved of the crooners who sang sophisticated songs during the late 1920s and early 1930s. Other singers of importance were Rudy Vallee (he was the first singer to use a public address system), Kate Smith and Russ Colombo. Crosby, however, was supreme, and this supremacy as a solo vocalist was not to be challenged until Frank Sinatra left the Tommy Dorsey band.

Bing Crosby died in 1978 when in his seventies (it is uncertain whether he was born in 1901 or 1904). He had had a long and distinguished career as a solo singer and actor that had begun when he split from Paul Whitemen in 1930. His first star role in a film was in *College Humor* (1933), which was to be followed in the 1940s by the famous series of 'Road' pictures made with comedian Bob Hope (the first was *The Road to Singapore*, made in 1940). Crosby and Hope carried on a friendly feud over the years, much to the amusement of their fans. The most famous of Crosby's radio shows (he began broadcasting as a solo singer in 1931) was the Kraft Music Hall, which began in January 1936, and continued into the 1940s. His hit songs are almost countless, and include such favourites as 'Galway Bay', 'San Antonio Rose', 'Pennies from Heaven', 'I've Got a Pocketful of Dreams' and 'Swinging on a Star'.

Ol' Blue Eyes When Sinatra left Tommy Dorsey, in September 1942, he went to Hollywood to try to get a job as a staff singer for NBC (one of the big broadcasting corporations). He was not successful, and managed instead to land a short, three-minute appearance singing a Cole Porter song ('Night and Day') in a Hollywood musical (*Reveille with Beverly*). After completing the film, Sinatra returned to New York in late December to appear at the Paramount Theater. The star of the show he was appearing in was Benny Goodman. When Goodman introduced Sinatra, the young singer got an unbelievable reception. 'The sound that greeted me was absolutely deafening,' recalled Sinatra. 'It was a tremendous uproar . . . I was scared stiff. I couldn't move a muscle. Benny froze too.'

Sinatra, in short, had got sex appeal. Not since the death of Rudolph Valentino had American women reacted with such fervour to a male star. Sinatra's main appeal was to 'bobbysoxers', as white teenage girls were then called. Like the Beatles twenty years later, the young Sinatra seemed helpless, innocent, and a little bit open to attack from the big wide world. It was possibly this vulnerability which at the same time made him attractive to older, more sophisticated women. This sort of appeal is clearly shown in a song such as 'I Couldn't Sleep a Wink Last Night'. But whatever the reasons for his appeal, Sinatra had by early 1943 clearly established himself as America's leading white male singer, a position held for the previous ten years or so by Bing Crosby.

Sinatra's supremacy lasted until about 1947, when his popularity began to wane. One reason for this slide was overwork. A schedule which sometimes included forty-five concerts a week was bound to strain the singer's voice, and this strain began to

show. Another reason was that by 1947 the
newspapers were beginning to accuse Sinatra of
having connections with organised crime in the
shape of the Mafia. These unproved allegations have
dogged Sinatra all his life.

But perhaps the main reason for Sinatra's
declining popularity lay with Sinatra himself. As a
man, Sinatra has been generous almost to a fault.
When the actor Lee J. Cobb suffered a heart attack,
for example, Sinatra paid the hospital bills and then
let the actor recover in his Palm Springs and
Hollywood homes. Sinatra was also not afraid to
stand up for people who were being hard done by. In
1945, when such topics were still very touchy,
Sinatra made a film (*The House I Live In*) criticising
white attitudes to black people. But like other men
who are generous and protective, Sinatra was also
fiercely independent. He wanted to succeed *his* way
and on *his* terms, a fact later reflected in his hit song
'My Way'.

Among Sinatra's terms was that his public and
private lives should remain separate. Because
Sinatra had made it to the top without any real help
from newspapers and publicity men, he felt that he
did not owe them anything. Newspapermen felt
rather differently, however. Anything any big
personality did had news value, and Sinatra was no
exception, particularly where his relationships with
women were concerned. As well as being attractive
to women, Sinatra has also been easily attracted by
them. He has been married four times, and also had
a number of affairs. Because, as his second wife Ava
Gardner has said, Sinatra 'is highly sensitive and
intelligent,' and because he felt he did not owe
newspapermen anything, he became easily angry at
their constant attentions. This anger on one occasion

spilled over into physical violence. Sinatra's problems with the news media have been beautifully summed up by the actor Humphrey Bogart. 'Sinatra's idea of Paradise is a place where there are plenty of women and no newspapermen,' he said. 'He doesn't know it,' Bogart went on, 'but he'd be better off if it were the other way round.'

The news media are very important to any big personality. They can present personalities to the public in a good light or a bad light. Because of Sinatra's attitude, he was frequently presented in a bad light. Together with voice problems, marriage problems, and accusations over the Mafia, Sinatra's bad Press relations gradually destroyed his career. By 1952, he was finished. He had no recording contract, no film contract and no radio sponsors.

Sinatra's comeback is extraordinary for two reasons. First, it is unheard of for anyone to come back from a ruined career with the success of Sinatra. Second, Sinatra's comeback was not made as a singer, but as an actor. After a great deal of badgering, Sinatra managed to persuade the head of a big Hollywood studio to let him play Private Maggio in the film *From Here To Eternity*. The singer was a great success in a part which had no singing in it at all. One reason was that the character Maggio had an Italian–American background similar to that of Sinatra. Sinatra had, in fact, been brought up in a multi-racial district of Hoboken, a small town in New Jersey where children looked after themselves by using their fists. As Sinatra said, 'I knew Maggio. I went to high school with him in Hoboken. I was beaten up with him. I might have been Maggio.'

Another reason for Sinatra's success was that he obviously had hidden talent as an actor. After making *From Here To Eternity* – for which, in 1953, he was awarded an Oscar for the Best Supporting Performance (Male) – Sinatra had little trouble getting other film parts. His singing career also started to pick up as he began making long-playing records with arranger Nelson Riddle. The Sinatra–Riddle combination was to prove extremely successful, producing albums like *Songs For Young Lovers, The Wee Small Hours, Songs For Swinging Lovers, Only The Lonely* and *No One Cares.* By 1954, Sinatra had re-established himself not only as *the* top male singer, but also as a very good actor.

Sinatra began to work less hard during the 1970s. At the time of writing, his last feature film (*Dirty Dingus Magee*) had been made in 1970. He also 'retired' in 1971, but the retirement lasted only two-and-a-half years. As might be expected of a man entering his sixties, Sinatra's voice began to falter a little. This does not matter when making records, as it is possible to re-record a song until it sounds right. But even though the voice has occasionally given way during live performances, there can be little doubting the presence of the man. In 1977, at the age of sixty-two, Sinatra became the first solo artist ever to appear for an entire week at London's Albert Hall.

Until Sinatra became famous, Bing Crosby had undoubtedly been the most popular singer of this century. But Sinatra had two advantages over Bing Crosby. First, Crosby might have sounded as if 'he were leaning over the piano in your parlor singing to you.' In contrast to this, to many women in the mid-1940s it sounded as if Sinatra was trying to make love to them and to them alone through his singing. Second, Sinatra made better use of the microphone

The mature and
authoritative
Sinatra

than Crosby. It has been said that while Crosby was
overheard by the microphone, Sinatra 'played' or
sang on it. He quickly learnt which sounds worked
best over the microphone, and strove to cut out
those which did not.

But Sinatra's greatest advantage was his uncanny
sense of timing when delivering lyrics. This timing
rested on an ability to sing a melody as if it were one
unbroken phrase, an ability he got from Tommy

Dorsey and, a little surprisingly, the classical violinist Jascha Heifitz. Frank Sinatra has described this ability, as well as the way in which it made him different from other singers:

> The thing that influenced me most was the way Tommy played his trombone. He would take a musical phrase and play it all the way through without breathing, for eight, ten, maybe sixteen bars. How in the hell did he do it? Why couldn't a singer do that, too? Fascinated, I began listening to other soloists. I bought every Jascha Heifitz record I could find, and listened to him play the violin hour after hour. His constant bowing, where you never heard a break, carried the melody line straight on through, just like Dorsey's trombone. It was my idea to make my voice work in the same way as a trombone or violin – not sounding like them, but 'playing' the voice like those instruments . . . Instead of singing only two bars or four bars of music at a time – like most of the other guys around – I was able to sing six bars and, in some songs, eight bars without taking a visible or audible breath. This gave the melody a flowing, unbroken quality, and that – if anything – was what made me sound different.

Instead of making him sound like a trained singer, all these skills made Sinatra sound as if he were holding a personal conversation with you. And that is where his great artistry lies. For the clever use of the microphone, the careful stretching of notes, and the beautiful phrasing all serve to tell us about Sinatra the man. Over the years his fierceness and sadness, his toughness and tenderness have, through his singing, summed up the hopes and disappointments of millions of people. That is why, at the time of writing, Sinatra is the only popular entertainer who can really be called 'a legend in his own time'.

Frank Sinatra's success with the bobbysoxers is the climax of our story. For by the early 1950s, Tin Pan Alley as it has been described in this book was beginning to go into decline. The decline is discussed in chapter 10. Before then, however, we will take a look at what was happening in Britain while Tin Pan Alley was reigning supreme in America.

9 Fighting the menace

Introduction   So far, this book has described the main events in the history of white commercial popular music *in America*. Why has so much time been spent on America, and none on Britain? There are two answers to this question. First, once Tin Pan Alley came into being, British popular music stopped having any influence on American. Not until the Beatles became popular in 1963 did Americans really take any notice of what was happening in Britain. The second answer is that American popular music gradually spread around the world. By the 1920s, white American popular music had become part of the popular music of many other countries, including Britain.

But although American popular music became very important to British popular entertainment, it was disliked by many British people, especially those belonging to the middle classes. This chapter discusses the spread of American popular music ('the menace') to Britain, and the way that much British popular music managed to keep going in spite of it ('the fight').

The menace   One reason for this spread of American popular music was that America fought two world wars in Europe. As her soldiers crossed the Atlantic, so did

Glenn Miller in England, 1944

her popular music. We have seen how Jim Europe took his 'army' band to France in February 1918, and how Glenn Miller and his 'army' band came to Britain in 1944.

Hollywood also had a great deal to do with making American commercial music popular outside America. Chapter 6 described how nearly all the early Hollywood films were musicals. Once made and put into their metal canisters, these films could easily be sent abroad. It was a flood of such films which finally put paid to British music hall and revue in the early 1930s, for example. Records as well have played their part in the spread of American popular music. We saw in chapter 5 how American record companies were quick to see the profit in recording popular music. English record companies, on the other hand, were much more interested in recording classical and 'light' music, and paid hardly any attention to American popular music. As a result, the American companies had little competition when it came to selling their music abroad.

White American popular music also spread abroad easily because it was different from the popular music of any other country. This book has described how Tin Pan Alley took over many types of Afro-American music and used them for its own ends. Ragtime, the blues, jazz and Swing all became Alley fashions. Furthermore, the singing of the ballad, the staple diet of Tin Pan Alley, was also influenced by the Afro-American tradition. This tradition has given much white American popular music an air of excitement and a hint of mystery which many people, including non-Americans, have found hard to resist.

But why did British music stop having any influence? The main reason was that British popular songs and their singers came to be very parochial (that is, tied to a particular place and local interests). As Ed Lee points out in *Folksong and Music Hall*, British people were very attached to their own areas and their own class of people, and it showed in the lyrics of their songs. Marie Lloyd, who dominated English music hall for the first twenty years of this century, had a song that went as follows, for example:

> I'd like to go to Paris on the Seine
> For Paris is a proper pantomime,
> And if they'd only shift the 'Ackney Road
> And plant it over there
> I'd like to live in Paris all the time.

America, on the other hand, was far from settled. Many people had lost their roots, either because they had recently moved to a city from the country, or because they had recently come from a country overseas. For this reason, their songs could not be parochial. People from different cultures do not always understand each other very easily, and so they talk about what they have in common: hopes, disappointments, families and loves. This is what the Tin Pan Alley song has nearly always been about, and this is another reason why the American ballad has travelled so easily to other countries.

Britain, too, had a Tin Pan Alley. Situated around Denmark Street in London, it spent most of its time selling the sheet music of songs successful in music hall. Like its American counterpart, it began to suffer when records and radio came along. The sales of sheet music went down, and music hall began to go into a decline. British song-writers also had their own professional association in the form of the Performing Rights Society, founded in 1914. Like ASCAP in America, the Performing Rights Society collected royalties from recorded or live performances and then handed them on to its members.

The British Alley followed a similar path to the one in America. However, it was not long before it felt the influence of its cousin across the Atlantic. American selling techniques were soon in evidence. In 1923, for example, the song 'Yes, We Have No Bananas' was advertised by giving away free bananas. And in 1927 the publisher Lawrence Wright advertised 'Me and Jane in a Plane' by having a band fly over Blackpool playing the song. Lawrence Wright was the most successful of British publishers. He was quick to realise the importance of the American popular song, and signed up Walter Donaldson, the composer of 'My Blue Heaven' (see chapter 6). Like Berlin, Gershwin and others, Donaldson had a great deal of success in Britain with his songs during the 1920s and early 1930s.

It was in 1912 that the invasion really started. In this year a revue, *Hello Ragtime*, opened at the London Hippodrome. (A revue is basically the same as vaudeville or music hall, except that the different acts are linked by a theme – in this case, ragtime.) The revue was a great success, running for some 451 performances, and establishing ragtime as a new and sensational entertainment fashion in Britain. One of the most popular songs of the day was Irving Berlin's 'Alexander's Ragtime Band'.

As in America, ragtime was followed by jazz in the shape of the ODJB. The band came to England in 1919 and first performed in a revue, *Joy Bells*, which was being put on (once again) at the London Hippodrome. The ODJB were an immediate sensation, getting more applause than the show's star, famous music hall entertainer George Robey. Robey said that either the band had to leave the show, or he would. As a result, the ODJB found themselves out of work. This did not last for long, however. The tour was very successful, especially for Nick LaRocca, who is supposed to have got into trouble chasing the daughters of wealthy English gentlemen.

Jazz in Britain took two directions. A minority, mainly university students, became genuinely interested in jazz as a result of the ODJB visit. The students gradually learnt about real black jazz, and some of them travelled to America to hear it and to buy records. Perhaps the best-known Englishman to be excited by American jazz at the time was the journalist Alistair Cooke, later to become famous for his radio programme, 'Letter From America'.

For the majority, however, jazz quickly became the same thing as dance music, especially after Paul Whiteman visited England in 1923. Many English 'jazz' bands were formed in the 1920s. One of the best known was led by Jack Hylton, and it was this band which flew over Blackpool playing 'Me and Jane in a Plane'.

Bands such as Hylton's (others were Ambrose and His Orchestra and the Savoy Orpheans) played mainly in the posh London dance-clubs which opened their doors before the First World War and continued to flourish afterwards. They also played in restaurants and night-clubs. It was in these plush Mayfair venues that American dancing was introduced. The Charleston, for example, was a craze that lasted for just two years in the 1920s, to be followed by the less successful Black Bottom.

The coming of American dances (many of which were introduced to London society by Irene Castle) threw many people into confusion. Some people, for example, thought that 'the Jazz' was actually a dance. Only two American dances made a lasting impression, however. They were the Foxtrot and the Quickstep (a fast Foxtrot). These, plus two others, became the mainstay of British ballroom dancing. The other two were the tango, an exotic Latin-American dance which had come to Britain via America, and the waltz. The waltz was no longer the stiff, starchy and fast affair it had been when it first came from Vienna, but a more relaxed and slower dance that allowed closer contact between couples. The grouping of British ballroom dancing into four main dances was first carried out in about 1924 by the Imperial Society of Teachers of Dancing. It was part of an attempt to make British Ballroom dancing more restrained and respectable than its American counterpart, an attempt greatly helped by the work of Victor Sylvester, Britain's most famous and successful dance teacher.

The 'Pony-Trot'
invades England
in 1920!

The Charleston being danced in London, 1926

As a pastime, ballroom dancing gradually became popular with people other than the upper classes in Britain. The first of the big public ballrooms, the Hammersmith Palais de Dance, was opened in 1919. Others soon followed, and by the 1930s millions were going ballroom dancing every week. Ballroom dancing became a very cheap form of entertainment. However, until the Second World War it was the upper crust and expensive Mayfair night-clubs and dance-clubs which set the trends.

Another cheap form of entertainment for the majority of people was to be found in the cinema. Cinemas in Britain became established during the First World War. They showed mainly Hollywood silent movies and, as in America, these films were accompanied on the piano, the organ, or occasionally by an orchestra. Talking pictures arrived in 1927, and were as quick to catch on in Britain as they were in their native America. By the end of the 1930s (Hollywood's golden decade), more than half the population of Britain was going to the pictures each week.

The cinema and the 'palais de dance' provided the British with their two main forms of entertainment during the 1930s. As a result, they also provided them with their main sources of popular music. Not surprisingly, American popular music tended to dominate the English. This domination continued despite the fact that English ballroom dancing developed a style that was more polite and restrained than the American (it was known as the 'English style'), and that quite a few films were made in Britain.

With the coming of the Second World War the American domination of British popular music became greater. After December 1941, thousands of

American troops were stationed in Britain. They brought with them Swing music in the form of *V-discs*. These records were given away free to troops by the American government, and continued to be made even during the AFoM strike of 1942–3. Swing music started to be imitated in Britain, particularly by bands like the Squadronnaires, who were sponsored by the British forces.

As well as music, American servicemen also brought with them dances such as the jitterbug, as well as a good deal of money. Their music, their dancing, their livelier attitude to life, and above all their money made them attractive to many British women. This unfortunately caused some jealousy among British servicemen. It was often said of American servicemen during the war that they were 'over-fed, over-sexed and over here'.

After the Second World War, crooners became very popular in Britain, especially Frank Sinatra. On one occasion the British jazz musician John Dankworth was mistaken for Sinatra, and mobbed by a crowd of teenage girls. However, the British had their own answers to American crooners. Artists such as Alma Cogan and Dennis Lotis made their own versions of American popular songs, while singers such as Anne Shelton and David Whitfield recorded middle-of-the-road, pleasant ballads.

Britain also had one outstanding answer to American Swing bands. Ted Heath, a trombone section man of long standing, formed his band during the war. However, it was after the war that the band really came into its own. Heath ran a fortnightly show called 'Sunday Night at the London Palladium' which continued for many years. In 1955, he also took his band on the first of a series of American tours. The band turned out to be as popular in America as it

opposite
Ted Heath 'swings' his trombone in the air to signal the end of a show in Wolverhampton

was in Britain, and this was no mean feat at the time.

The fight English popular music managed to keep going and in some cases to thrive during the period 1900–50. A very important reason for this was that English popular music of the first half of this century was *extremely* English. We have already mentioned Marie Lloyd, for example, and her appeal, which really ended on the outskirts of London. Another important strand of the English tradition was music made for the middle classes. Ed Lee, in *Folk Song and Music Hall*, has described such music up to about 1914. But the tradition continued after that date. Perhaps the most important composers were Noel Coward, who is probably most famous for his comic songs such as 'Mad Dogs and Englishmen' and 'Don't Put Your Daughter on the Stage, Mrs Worthington', and Ivor Novello, who wrote theatre music, such as the ballad 'We'll Gather Lilacs'.

The appeal of Gracie Fields and George Formby was also very English, but in a totally different way. Both these entertainers came from Lancashire, and at the beginnings of their careers they usually played to working-class audiences in the north of England. George Formby was famous for his ukulele playing. The ukulele is a twangy, guitar-like instrument on which the entertainer used to accompany himself while singing. Formby was also famous for his earthy humour. In some ways the north was (and still is) to the south of England what the south of the United States was (and still is) to the north there. The north of England was not as sophisticated as areas round London. It was heavily industrialised, and people were thus much closer to the harsh realities of life –

opposite
George Formby
in 'fighting' mood! to long hours of back-breaking work, to poverty, sickness and unexpected death. One of the ways

they kept cheerful was to joke about these harsh realities in an honest way. Many people in the south found this kind of humour distasteful. How, for example, could you joke about a corpse in bed, or the naughty things a window cleaner might see ('When I'm Cleaning Windows')? The BBC (of whom we shall talk in a moment) asked George Formby to clean up some of the lines in his songs when he went south to do radio shows. Formby was very offended. It was true that he had a rough-and-ready way of delivering his songs, and that his humour was direct. But he had always thought of his acts as family acts. The thousands of families who had queued up to see him on stage were evidence of this.

Gracie Fields also became famous outside her native north. However, her music and humour always had its roots there. She never sang her best-known song ('The Biggest Aspidistra in the World') in anything but a Lancashire accent, for example. She also never let her singing become over-emotional. It was all right to be sentimental or even sad. But although people in the north might have it harder than people in the south, they should never break down and feel sorry for themselves. After all, people in the north were tougher.

The most successful English popular singer of the first half of this century was Vera Lynn. Her singing style was very different from that of Gracie Fields and George Formby. While Gracie Fields had a powerful way of singing, Vera Lynn's style was smoother, softer, more melodious, and certainly more acceptable to the middle classes. The singer was everybody's idea of the 'English rose' that English girls are supposed to be. She had a voice that was as clear as a bell, a radiant complexion, and was

opposite
The 'English rose', Vera Lynn, broadcasting to the troops in 1945

attractive rather than beautiful. Vera Lynn's success can be summed up in one phrase. She was the 'Forces' Sweetheart'. During the Second World War she sang songs over the radio to troops abroad which reminded them of their families and their sweethearts. One of her best-known songs was 'The White Cliffs of Dover'. These cliffs were the sight that many a British soldier would have seen on returning home from the fighting in Europe.

British radio was notable for not broadcasting popular music in the same way as American radio. Being a more democratic country (at least as far as white people were concerned), America let its people hear what they wanted to on the radio. Programmes were commercially sponsored, and the sponsors, of course, were keen to attract audiences. In Britain, on the other hand, radio was financed *by the government* through licence fees collected from everyone who owned a receiving set. There were no adverts, no sponsors, and so no way in which public taste could have some influence over what was broadcast. First given a licence to broadcast in 1923, the BBC (at first called the British Broadcasting *Company*, and later the British Broadcasting *Corporation*) gave people what it thought they ought to be listening to rather than what they actually wanted. In doing this, the BBC reflected the strong class divisions in Britain. The upper and middle classes had most of the power. As a result, they naturally wanted to influence and, if possible, control the activities and interests of everybody else.

Most BBC programmes in the early days were made up either of classical music (appealing mainly to the middle classes), or of talks which were intellectual or 'educational', and thus likely to be of interest only to the middle and upper classes. Since the BBC had a monopoly on radio broadcasting until the 1970s (this meant that no one else was allowed to broadcast radio programmes), it was difficult to tune in to a different station and hear other kinds of music. The only real alternative was provided by Radio Luxembourg, which began broadcasting pre-recorded British and American popular music from the small European state of Luxembourg in the 1930s.

The BBC did allow some popular music in the early days, but this music was usually the very polite kind of dance music played by English bands. In 1923, for example, the BBC invited Henry Hall to form the BBC Dance Orchestra. Henry Hall

Henry Hall, the epitome of English reserve!

presented the Dance Orchestra's broadcasts in a clipped, upper-class accent. The music suited the accent. It was smooth, subdued, sophisticated and as far removed as possible from the kind of music first made popular by the ODJB. Hall's programmes were, however, popular with all kinds of British people.

The BBC's attitude to popular music continued until the 1960s. Then, however, 'pirate' radio stations started broadcasting 'pop' music in Britain. These stations (the most famous was Radio Caroline) were on ships anchored at sea, and thus outside British law. The BBC was forced to compete with them. It therefore reorganised its three radio channels into four, and started broadcasting 'pop' music. The real importance of the BBC to our story, however, is that it encouraged the idea that most popular music, and *especially* American popular music, was somehow nasty and undesirable. It was not the sort of music that the politely spoken, 'nice' young men who announced BBC programmes would have liked. The BBC played a very important part in 'fighting the menace'.

English popular music after the Second World War continued to be pleasant and polite. Alma Cogan and David Whitfield worked for the BBC, for example. But in the early 1950s, a group of people grew up who were far from pleasant and polite. 'Teddy boys', as they were known, dressed in long velvet jackets, drainpipe trousers and pointed shoes. They were largely working-class teenage boys who wandered round in gangs, sometimes terrorising ballrooms, cinemas and innocent passers-by. Teddy boys got their idea from watching Hollywood cowboy films. Their model was the typical 'baddy', the city 'gentleman' who wore long black coats, thin black trousers, pointed cowboy boots, had his greasy hair brushed back, and had grown thick sideburns.

When they first came into being, however, Teddy boys had no music of their own. For a music as aggressive as themselves, they had to wait until rock 'n' roll burst on the scene in late 1954. When rock 'n' roll did arrive it meant the end for Tin Pan Alley as we have come to know it in this book.

10 After the ball

The decline of Tin Pan Alley

The ASCAP–BMI dispute referred to in chapter 8 sowed the seeds for the decline of Tin Pan Alley as the major force in the production and marketing of white popular music. With few exceptions, the white city dwellers of the northern states had until 1941 heard only the music of white, city song-writers. Nearly all the song-writers whose music was played over the radio belonged to ASCAP. Irving Berlin, George Gershwin and all the main Broadway composers were members, for example. As we saw in chapter 6, many of them received some training in classical music. As a result, BMI was forced to buy up the music of urban song-writers not thought good enough to join the ranks of ASCAP. But, more importantly, BMI had to buy up and broadcast music that did not originate with white urban song-writers.

The two most important kinds were country and western music and rhythm and blues. Country music, the music of poor white southern country folk, grew out of the English, Scottish, Welsh and Irish folk music that settlers had brought with them to America between the seventeenth and nineteenth centuries. Rhythm and blues, on the other hand, developed from the rural blues. Although more sophisticated than the rural blues, rhythm and blues were still very gutsy, and still contained a strong sexual element.

Because of this, white radio stations were forced to broadcast copies (or 'covers') of rhythm and blues made by white musicians. These covers had more polite lyrics and the music itself sounded much more clean and respectable.

By the early 1950s, young white Americans had become tired of these very cleaned-up 'cover' versions and were beginning to demand something more exciting. This demand was met by rock 'n' roll, a white music that was a mixture of rhythm and blues, and country and western. Rock 'n' roll finally arrived in 1954, when Bill Haley and His Comets recorded 'Rock Around the Clock'. Some people thought rock 'n' roll would never last. This proved not to be the case, however. From 1954 onwards, the ballads of Tin Pan Alley would take second place to successive waves of rock music.

There are many reasons for the rise of rock 'n' roll, and these are discussed by Dave Rogers in *Rock 'n' Roll*. However, the way for rock 'n' roll was undoubtedly prepared through broadcasts of country music and 'cover' versions of rhythm and blues. And since these broadcasts would not have been possible without the ASCAP–BMI dispute, that dispute is very important to the decline of Tin Pan Alley. Once the floodgates were open to non-ASCAP music, there was no looking back. For Tin Pan Alley 'the ball was over'.

The Nabob of Sob   The period from about 1947 (when Frank Sinatra's popularity began to decline) through to 1955 (when rock 'n' roll made such an impact) was an uneasy one for commercial popular music. There was, however, one singer who bridged the gap between Sinatra on the one hand, and rock 'n' roll and Elvis Presley on the other. That singer was Johnny Ray.

Born in Dallas, in 1927, John Alvin Ray had the misfortune, at the age of ten, to lose half his hearing. In his own words, this turned him into 'just about the loneliest kid in the world', and it was this loneliness that he expressed through his singing. But instead of expressing it through carefully phrased lyrics, as Sinatra would have done, he expressed it through his stage act. Ray did not simply stand there, as the more conservative crooners did. He hunched himself up, staggered round the stage, dropped to his knees, gasped for breath, and, as often as not, burst into tears in an effort to get his message across. Relying on these actions rather than on his mediocre voice, Johnny Ray quickly earnt himself titles such as 'The Nabob of Sob', 'The Prince of Wails' and 'Cry Guy'.

Ray was influenced to some extent by black singers. However, his real importance to the history of commercial popular music lay in his stage act. After his success, no singer could afford to just stand on the stage and sing (if he wanted to appeal to young people, that is). The stage image became all important. One has only to think of Elvis Presley in the 1950s, for example, Mick Jagger in the 1960s (Mick Jagger is the lead singer of the Rolling Stones), or Rod Stewart in the 1970s.

Johnny Ray was more successful in Britain than he was in America, where he was thought of as something of a 'freak'. But in both countries he reflected the 'plight' of young people – alone and misunderstood by an older generation that had just finished fighting the Second World War. Through songs such as 'Cry' and 'The Little White Cloud That Cried', Ray gave vent to their feelings. As he said, 'through a miracle of faith and the Divine powers that

opposite
The Nabob of
Sob

have guided my emotional and spiritual life I can bring something to the kids who love me. I guess I'm a symbol or something to them.'

Johnny Ray reflected the disease, not the cure. With Ray, young people were complaining. With rock 'n' roll they were doing something about it. That, however, is another story.

Conclusions   Although Tin Pan Alley began to take second place to different forms of rock music in 1955, it did not go out of business altogether. There always has been – and it seems there always will be – room for the ballad and the ballad singer. Fashions change and singers change, but the formula remains the same: a well-written song, appealing to the general public's emotions, sung by an artist who can put over the song's message with conviction. Two of the most successful ballad singers of the 1960s and 1970s were Shirley Bassey and Tom Jones. Both come from Wales, and both have worked a great deal in Las Vegas, the gambling capital of the United States. Song-writers continue to be successful, too. One of the best-known names of the 1960s and 1970s was Burt Bacharach, a Canadian. Working in the United States he produced a great number of popular songs, among them 'Raindrops Keep Fallin' On My Head' for the film *Butch Cassidy and the Sundance Kid*.

Hollywood has not stopped making film musicals either. Although it is very different in style from 1930s' film musicals, *Grease* (released in 1978, and starring John Travolta and Olivia Newton-John) is a production that the old-style Hollywood film-makers would have been proud of. The success of the film helped promote the film's songs both on the radio and in the record shops. Conversely, the success of the songs in the charts helped promote the film. Once again, the formula has not changed.

Finally, the music of Tin Pan Alley has had an influence on a number of rock musicians. The Beatles, for example, have been responsible for many memorable ballads (such as 'Penny Lane', 'Yesterday', and 'The Fool on the Hill') which can be said to appeal to the public in much the same way as the sentimental ballads described earlier in the book. Since their break-up, Paul McCartney has carried on this side of their song-writing with his group Wings. Their most successful songs, 'Mull of Kintyre', for example, show many of the characteristics of the sentimental ballad.

The basic aim of this book has been to describe the big personalities and main events in the history of Tin Pan Alley from about 1895 to 1955. It has not, of course, been possible to include everyone and everything. However, many important themes and trends have come to light:

1 Tin Pan Alley was above all in business to make a profit. To do this, it constantly needed to get hold of new and exciting sources of music (such as ragtime and jazz). Having done this, however, it had to make such music acceptable to white audiences.
2 Like other business concerns, Tin Pan Alley was quick to exploit new media, particularly radio. When radio was invented, Tin Pan Alley made sure that it had a big say in what was broadcast. This in turn meant it had an equally big say in what the public was able to hear, as well as in how song-writers produced their music.
3 However, in order to make a profit, Tin Pan Alley

also needed to reflect people's concerns and changing social attitudes. In so doing, it to some extent furthered the demand for greater freedom on the part of black people, women and the young. But because it did reflect changing social attitudes, Tin Pan Alley had to alter fashion every time big social or historical events changed the nature of people's lives.

The story of Tin Pan Alley remains important for one over-riding reason. White American popular music and white American popular entertainment as a whole have spread throughout much of the world. They have done more than most people realise to change attitudes. We have seen, for example, how many British people looked down on popular American entertainment and tried to keep it at bay. Yet to many people in Britain, especially the less well-off, American music and American entertainment were like a breath of fresh air. They seemed open, exciting and free, and thus so unlike the rigid class system that gripped the country at least until the 1960s.

Has the power and influence of white American popular music been to the good? That is a question that people really have to answer for themselves. Tin Pan Alley was (and still is) highly commercial. It has taken over other people's music, changed it, and used it for its own ends. Because of this, many people have criticised it. Lovers of jazz, for example, usually feel that Tin Pan Alley has always corrupted their music and taken away its good qualities – that Tin Pan Alley never really gives the public 'real' jazz.

However, whether we approve of a type of music or not, different types of music exist, and do so because different kinds of people exist. Classical music, for example, tends to mirror the respectability and seriousness of the middle classes. Much rock music expresses the discontent of younger people who would like to see certain things in the world changed. In its past, Tin Pan Alley, too, has expressed the discontent of young people, although not in such a serious fashion. However, as time has passed, the music of Tin Pan Alley has simply become respectable light entertainment for all ages and classes, and has not attempted to say very much about the world into which it was born. After the Swing period, for example, young people looked elsewhere for music to reflect their discontents.

Some people would again criticise Tin Pan Alley music for this. They feel that the purpose of music should always be serious. However, many people would say that there is a time to be serious, and a time to relax, let the world pass by, and gain a little happiness when life is hard. For such people there will always be a place for the music of the Alley.

Glossary of musical terms

arrangement An *arranger* produces a version of an existing piece of music for performance by a particular combination of musicians (unlike a *composer*, who creates new pieces of music). In making an *arrangement* he may merely put it into suitable *notation*, add *harmony*, make an *orchestration*, or he may make considerable changes, so as to give the music his personal interpretation (as in, for example, the arrangements of Glenn Miller).

art-form (*or* 'serious art-form') Musical creations which are intended for attentive listening, and which have a serious purpose, rather than being designed as entertainment or background music.
(Compare **classical music**, and for further detail see *Folksong and Music Hall*, pp. 48–54.)

ballad This word has several meanings. In this book it means: (1) A short popular song. (2) A song of the nineteenth and twentieth centuries, which is more concerned with the feelings of the singer than with telling a story. (3) A song concerned with powerful, idealistic, unrealistic, and usually sad emotions.

bar Most Western music has a basic beat (often known as the pulse) to which you can tap your foot or dance. This pulse usually runs in a repeated pattern of 'strong' (louder) beats and 'weak' (softer) beats; this is known as the metre. In *Afro-American* music the commonest pattern (or *metre*) is: ONE two three four / ONE two three four, etc. One count of four is known as a *bar*. Other counts, such as three or five, can be used. These are also known as bars.

bass The lowest-pitched part in a piece of music. *String bass (double bass)* A stringed instrument used for playing bass parts. In appearance like a large, upright violin.

bending of notes   Sliding into or away from the central pitch of a note. This technique was used by many blues singers and instrumentalists. Later it found its way into the singing of white vocalists such as Al Jolson and Bing Crosby.

blue note   Blues musicians use a **scale** different from that traditionally used by classical musicians. The notes which were different were therefore often thought to be strange, wrong, or out of tune. These notes became known as *blue notes*.

Cakewalk   A dance of Afro-American origin which became very popular in about 1900. It was performed to *ragtime* and similar music. It resembled a strutting walk, and was originally created in imitation of white employers in the southern United States, during the second half of the nineteenth century.

call-and-response form   A method of music making in which a leader (possibly *improvising*) sings a line (the *call*), and is answered by a chorus (the *response*). The call and response are usually one line long each. This procedure is an important feature of African and Afro-American music.

chord   The result of sounding three or more different notes together.

classical music   A form of music created in Europe, or under a strong European influence, and preserved in musical notation. It is normally intended for attentive listening, either in concerts, or in religious ceremonies. Classical pieces tend to be of some length, and the composer pays special attention to problems of musical form. Though there are many modern composers of 'classical' or 'serious' music, the term is most often applied to music created before 1900. *Note*: The term 'Classical music' (with a capital C) is being used correctly only when it is applied to a particular style of the second half of the eighteenth century.

classic blues   Blues music created by black Americans in the cities between about 1920 and 1935, and including a strong jazz influence.

cornet   An instrument similar to a trumpet, but with a softer tone. It was popular in brass and military bands, and under the influence of the latter was adopted by many New Orleans jazz musicians.

country and western music   The music which was most

popular with white people in the southern states of the USA after about 1920. (For further details see *Rock 'n' Roll* pp. 22–9.)

folk music The popular music of one community. In practice, the music of rural societies of the past. Folk music was usually sung, and was passed on by ear. It was felt to be the property of all, and not just of one person.

Foxtrot (*also* Slow Foxtrot) A twentieth-century ballroom dance in four-beat time, similar to a Quickstep, but much slower in speed.

harmony (1) The 'harmony (or harmonies) of a tune' are the **chords** which accompany it. (2) When musicians study harmony, they study the *rules governing the use of chords*. (3) To 'harmonise' a tune is to fit harmonies to it.

improvisation This word has several meanings. In this book it means: (1) The act of composing music at the moment of performance, rather than planning it beforehand. (2) (With reference to jazz.) The on-the-spot composition of new lines of music or very free versions of the melody. This is in contrast to *ornamentation*, in which a relatively small number of notes are added to a tune to obtain variety and expressiveness. Such ornamentation may also be *planned in advance*.

key Most classical and popular music is said to be in a *key* (e.g. the key of C). This means that a particular **scale**, and the **chords** which can be derived from it are used. More important, one note will be of greater importance than all the others (the note after which the key is named). The whole piece of music will move towards this note, especially at the end of the piece. There are twelve major keys and twelve minor keys. F sharp major is considered to be one of the most difficult to work in. Thus the fact that Irving Berlin could only play in F sharp major meant that, compared to professional musicians he was very limited. Yet, strangely, he could work instinctively in a key which, because of its difficulties, is comparatively rarely used.

lead trumpet The player in a trumpet **section** who plays the chord notes of the highest pitch, and so decides on how to interpret the music. (Similarly, lead saxophone, lead trombone.)

lyric The words of a song.

maxixe   (This is a Portuguese-Brazilian word, pronounced ma-*she*-shay.) A dance from Brazil which became popular in the early years of this century.

measured pace   A steady speed, and not too fast.

minstrel show   A popular entertainment of the nineteenth century, based on the music, dancing and humour of black Americans. Such shows could be performed by white people wearing black make-up, or by black people themselves. (For details see *Folksong and Music Hall*, pp. 73–82; *Tin Pan Alley*, pp. 19–23; *Jazz and Blues*, pp. 22–3.)

music hall   A place of entertainment, with mostly working-class audiences, popular in Britain between about 1820 and 1920. The performance would include singers, comedians and other variety artists, such as magicians and jugglers.

notation   This term can be used in slightly different ways and can mean: (1) printed or written copies of pieces of music; (2) a system of writing down music; (3) the act of writing down music.

phrase   Several notes which make up a very short tune.

phrasing   The interpretation of a phrase (by playing louder/softer, shorter/longer, smoother/rougher, etc.) to give it expressiveness and meaning.

popular music   Any music which is liked by a very large number of people (a mass audience). Usually, but not always, the musical taste of the majority. Popular music is also often defined, in contrast to **classical music**, as music for which a special training is not needed. This is not strictly correct, but it is true to say that popular music is music which is not normally studied in the music education system (e.g. in music colleges).

pop music   The music favoured by young people (under 25) since about 1955. The term includes rock 'n' roll, reggae, Tamla Motown, etc.

Quickstep   A twentieth-century ballroom dance in a quick four-beat time, in which couples hold each other close, and the man leads in performing intricate steps.

rhythm and blues   The popular music of urban black Americans from about 1940 to 1960, and derived from the blues. (For further details see *Jazz and Blues*, pp. 116–118.)

scale   A set of pitches, most commonly arranged in ascending order, out of which musical tunes or compositions are made.

section   A group of musicians in a jazz big band, who all play the same instruments, and usually at the same time.

sheet music   Copies of short pieces of music, usually popular songs, with a piano accompaniment.

speciality act   A performance by an individual artist in a variety of *vaudeville* show. It was so called because the artist specialised in some skill (e.g. juggling or dancing).

swing   (1) The rhythmic effect obtained by jazz bands between about 1915 and 1965, or by bands after that date playing in an older style. (2) Swing (with capital S) is the name given to big band jazz and popular music, which enjoyed its greatest popularity during the 1930s and early 1940s.

syncopation   (1) Strictly speaking, *syncopation* refers to a rhythmic stress that is deliberately misplaced. In syncopation, the stresses in one or more lines of the music are different from those of the basic pattern (or *metre* – see **bar**), and clash with them. (2) Especially with reference to earlier jazz, people often said that the music was 'syncopated'. By this they meant not only that an occasional note clashed with the basic *metre*, but that whole **phrases** did so. Also, such people were thinking of the fact that, unlike in most of the classical music they knew, jazz used this type of rhythmic effect *all the time*.

tango   A dance of Spanish and Latin-American origin in a moderate four-beat time, using exaggerated movements. It became popular in the early years of this century.

tuba   A large, brass instrument related to the trumpet, which provides a **bass**. It was greatly used in New Orleans jazz, and dance bands of the 1920s.

vaudeville   A form of American theatre entertainment between about 1895 and 1925, which presented variety acts and music. (For further details see pp. 23–5.)

vocal line   A line of music for a singer.

waltz   A very popular social dance of the nineteenth and twentieth centuries, in which the couples hold each other close, and dance steps in the order they choose. Originally it was a fairly quick German peasant dance in three-beat time, but it later became much slower. The Viennese Waltz is a form of quick waltz developed in Vienna in the nineteenth century. (For further details see *Folksong and Music Hall*, pp. 129–31.)

Wurlitzer organ   A type of very big electric organ which became popular after the First World War, and was often used in cinemas. It had many special effects, including chimes and percussion which could be operated by the organist at the same time as he played a more regular organ part. The name 'Wurlitzer' is a trade name.

Sources and acknowledgments

P. 1 Irving Caesar from Tony Palmer, *All You Need Is Love* (Futura, 1976); p. 2 Harry von Tilzer from Palmer, op. cit.; p. 3 lyrics of 'A Bird in a Gilded Cage' copyright B. Feldman & Co.; p. 6 lyrics from 'Yesterday' from Wilfrid Mellers, *Twilight of the Gods* (Faber, 1973); p. 6 Irving Caesar from Palmer, op. cit.; p. 6 Irving Caesar from Palmer, op. cit.; p. 9 Edward B. Marks from David Ewen, *All the Years of American Popular Music* (Prentice-Hall, 1977); p. 10 Bing Crosby from Palmer, op. cit.; p. 15 lyrics from 'The Old Folks at Home' from Richard Jackson, *Popular Songs of Nineteenth Century America* (Dover, 1976); p. 18 Shepherd N. Edmonds from Rudi Blesh and Harriet Janis, *They All Played Ragtime* (Oak Publications, 1971); p. 30 *New York Clipper* from Blesh and Janis, op. cit.; p. 31 Roy Carew from Blesh and Janis, op. cit.; p. 31 a publisher from Blesh and Janis, op. cit.; p. 36 *Metronome* from Blesh and Janis, op. cit.; p. 37 *Musical America* from Blesh and Janis, op. cit.; p. 37 president AMoF from Blesh and Janis, op. cit.; p. 37 *The Musician* from Blesh and Janis, op. cit.; p. 39 Vernon Castle from A. H. Franks, *Social Dance: A Short History* (Routledge & Kegan Paul, 1963); p. 40 Vernon Castle from Franks, op. cit.; p. 55 W. C. Handy from W. C. Handy, *Father of the Blues* (Sidgwick & Jackson, 1961); p. 58 Nick LaRocca from H. O. Brunn, *The Story of the Original Dixieland Jazz Band* (Sidgwick & Jackson, 1961); p. 58 *Variety* from H. O. Brunn, op. cit.; p. 59 Gilda Gray from H. O. Brunn, op. cit.; p. 60 Paul Whiteman from Albert McCarthy, *The Dance Band Era* (Studio Vista, 1971); p. 62 souvenir programme from McCarthy, op. cit.; p. 62 Gus Mueller from Neil Leonard, *Jazz and the White Americans* (University of Chicago Press, 1962); p. 62 Gus Mueller from Leonard, op. cit.; p. 63 lyrics from 'Johnny's in Town' from Ian Whitcomb, *After the Ball* (Penguin, 1972); p. 63 Paul Whiteman from Leonard, op. cit.; p. 64 Milton Mezzrow from Leonard, op. cit.; p. 64 *New York Times* from Leonard, op. cit.; p. 64 a journalist from Leonard, op. cit.; p. 64 a Princeton professor from Leonard, op. cit.; p. 68 *Etude* from Leonard, op. cit.; p. 69 a radio listener from Leonard, op. cit., p. 73 lyrics from 'My Blue Heaven' from Ian Whitcomb, *Tin Pan Alley: A Pictorial History (1919–1939)* (Paddington Press, 1975); p. 77 Rouben Mamoulian from Palmer, op. cit.; p. 87 Busby Berkeley from Tony Thomas and Jim Terry, *The Busby Berkeley Book* (Thames & Hudson, 1973); p. 88 Artie Shaw from Palmer, op. cit.; p. 91 Artie Shaw from Palmer, op. cit.; p. 91 Artie Shaw from Palmer, op. cit.; p. 103 Al Jolson from Henry Pleasants, *The Great American Popular Singers* (Gollancz, 1974); p. 104 Bing Crosby from Pleasants, op. cit.; p. 104 Rudy Vallee from Pleasants, op. cit.; p. 106 a radio announcer from Pleasants, op. cit.; p. 107 Frank Sinatra from Alan Frank, *Sinatra* (Hamlyn, 1978); p. 109 Ava Gardner from Frank, op. cit.; p. 110 Humphrey Bogart from Frank, op. cit.; p. 110 Frank Sinatra from Frank, op. cit.; p. 110 Sinatra from Pleasants, op. cit.; p. 117 lyrics from Marie Lloyd song from Whitcomb, *After the Ball* (Penguin, 1972); p. 136 Johnny Ray from 'Johnny Ray: Nabob of Sob', in *Story of Pop*, Vol. I (Phoebus Publishing, 1974); p. 136 Johnny Ray from *Story of Pop*, op. cit.

Pictures Pp. 15, 23, 41, 43, 44, 51, 63, 78, 81, 82, 85, 102, 112, 116, 122, 124, 129, 137, the Radio Times Hulton Picture Library; pp. 16, 20, 121, the Mansell Collection; pp. 66, 68, the Science Museum, London; pp. 105, 108, the National Film Archive; pp. 47, 53, Bill Greensmith; p. 131, Jazz Music Books; p. 75, EMI Music Publishers; p. 127, Popperfoto; p. 35, Peter Newark's Western Americana Picture Library. Author and publishers are grateful to the above for permission to reproduce copyright material.

Some suggestions for further reading and listening

Books The most readable account of the history of Tin Pan Alley is to be found in Ian Whitcomb, *After the Ball* (Penguin Books, 1972). The first three parts of this book deal with the development of the Alley (both in America and England) in a way that brings the atmospheres of different periods and fashions very vividly to life.

The most complete, general book on the history of American popular music is David Ewen, *All the Years of American Popular Music* (Prentice-Hall, 1977). The first five parts of this book are best used as a source of reference for specific topics.

The following books are more specialised in content, and should be used to expand knowledge on important personalities and topics. They are all well illustrated:

Rudi Blesh and Harriet Janis, *They All Played Ragtime* (Oak Publications, 1971). The authoritative book on ragtime.
Alan Frank, *Sinatra* (Hamlyn Publishing, 1978). An excellent, thoroughly illustrated account of Sinatra the man, as well as of Sinatra the singer, actor and entertainer.
Jonathon Green, *Glenn Miller and the Age of Swing* (Dempsey & Squires, 1976). A highly readable and thoroughly illustrated account of the Swing era and its most popular personality.
Stanley Green, *The World of Musical Comedy* (A. S. Barnes, 1960). This book contains short biographies of all the main Broadway composers and lyricists.
Albert McCarthy, *The Dance Band Era* (Studio Vista, 1970).
Albert McCarthy, *Big Band Jazz* (Barrie & Jenkins, 1974).

Both this and the above book will tell you anything you want to know about well-known jazz and dance bands, as well as the musicians who played in them.

Henry Pleasants, *The Great American Popular Singers* (Victor Gollancz, 1974). This book contains interesting discussions of the most important American popular singers and their art, as well as an important analysis of the main differences in technique to be found between classical singers and popular singers.

Recordings

Chapter	Title	Label	Number
Chapter 3	*The Scott Joplin Ragtime Album*	CBS	31497
Chapter 4	*The Young Irving Berlin*	EMI	SH 275
Chapter 5	*The Original Dixieland Jazz Band*	EMI	SH 220
Chapter 6	*The Music of Walter Donaldson*	EMI	SH 229
	Jerome Kern's 'Showboat'	EMI	SH 240
	Gershwin's Greatest Hits, Vol II	CBS	30090
	Presenting the Golden Age of the Hollywood Musical	UAG	29421
	Starring Fred Astaire	CBS	88062
Chapter 7	*Benny Goodman: A Legendary Performer*	RCA	PL 12470
	Benny Goodman Trio and Quartet	RCA	730.629
	Artie Shaw and His Orchestra, Vol I	RCA	FXMI 7336
	Glenn Miller: A Legendary Performer	RCA	DPM 2065
Chapter 8	*The Al Jolson Story: His Greatest Hits*	EMI	MCFM 2516
	Bing: A Musical Autobiography	EMI	CDMSP 801
	The Very Best of Frank Sinatra	EMI	E-ST 23256
Chapter 9	*Jack Hylton and His Orchestra*	EMI	SH 269
	The Alma Cogan Collection	EMI	OU 2168
	Focus on David Whitfield	Decca	FOS 57/58
	The Best of George Formby	EMI	OU 2072
	Vera Lynn: Hits of the Blitz	EMI	CSD 1457
	This Is Henry Hall	EMI	SHB 48
Chapter 10	*Tom Jones Live at Caesar's Palace*	EMI	MFP 5035
	Shirley Bassey 25th Anniversary	AG	SBTV 60147/48
	Burt Bacharach's Greatest Hits	A&M	AMLS 63661

Index

This is a name index only. Page numbers in italics at the end of entries refer to pictures.